Threads and Patches

Threads and Patches

Dr David Pearson MA (Oxon),
Hon D.Litt., FRSA.

JANUS PUBLISHING COMPANY LTD
Cambridge, England

First published in Great Britain 2021
by Janus Publishing Company Ltd
The Studio
High Green
Great Shelford
Cambridge CB22 5EG

www.januspublishing.co.uk

Copyright © David Pearson 2021
British Library Cataloguing-in-Publication Data
A catalogue record for this book is available from the British Library

ISBN 978-1-85756-917-9

All rights reserved. No part of this publication may be reproduced,
stored in a retrieval system or transmitted in any form or by any
means, electric, mechanical, photocopying, recording or otherwise,
without the prior permission of the publisher.

The right of David Pearson to be identified as the author
of this work has been asserted by him in accordance with the
Copyright, Designs and Patents Act 1988.

Cover Design: Janus Publishing

Cover Image: Supplied by the author

Printed and bound in Great Britain

Dedicated to my grandchildren
Bibiana, Luken and Tobias.
May they have as much fulfilment and enjoyment
in their lives as I have had in mine.

Luken, aged 2, Bibiana, aged 4, and Tobias, aged 3, in 2020.

Contents

Preface	xi
Introduction	xv
Part I: Career	1
Connections	3
Institutions	13
Manners Makyth Man	21
Part II: Happenings	27
A Cat Has Nine Lives	29
The Dentist's Chair	33
Namesakes	35
I Was There (or Thereabouts)	41
Travelling	47
Six Degrees of Separation	57
Part III: Diversions	67
Acting	69
Cowboys and Indians	73
Munich	77

Singing	83
Cricket	91
Messing About in Boats	97
Golf	105
Reading (and Writing)	111
Walking	117
Tennis	123

Part IV: Reflections and Observations — 127

My Blogs	129
History: Manchester Grammar School at 500	131
Politics and Economics: Small States	137
Current Affairs: Smoked Salmon	141
Foreign Affairs: The Chilean Way	147
Foreign Affairs: *Third Man in Havana*	151
Chile: Fine Wines from Chile	157
Environment and Sustainability: Global Goals	163
Technology and Innovation: Centre for Leadership Innovation	169
Marketing and Business: Duchy Originals	175
Board Governance: The Time I Interviewed Ruby Wax	181
Leadership and Management: The Importance of Failure	185
People and Networking: Desmond Tutu	191
The Worshipful Company of Marketors: The Year in Perspective	199
In Memoriam: Lord Montagu of Beaulieu	203
Education: A Mathematics Problem	207

Philanthropy: CANCERactive	211
Language and Culture: World Heritage List	215
Pedantry: It Doesn't Add Up	219
Sport: Slow Play	223
Future: The Threats and Opportunities of the Internet	229
The Perils of the Internet	235
Day One	243
Part V: Philosophy	**247**
Politics	249
Being Right	255
I've Got a Little List	259
Immortality	261

Preface

"A wandering minstrel, I
A thing of shreds and patches."

William Schwenk Gilbert

I started writing these notes/essays in 2001, and then in 2009 I started writing my blogs which I publish on my website, www.davidcpearson. co.uk. The two sets of writing had a different purpose. I originally wrote *Threads and Patches* for myself, though in the back of my mind I also thought that they could be left for posterity. As these essays and blogs were written as individual pieces rather than as a single narrative, there is sometimes a bit of repetition, for which I hope the reader will forgive me.

That sounds like a grand statement and is not intended to mean more than that for those who come after me who have any interest in how I spent my life, then here is at least some account of some of the themes and some of the adventures and some of the thrills and some of the pleasure that I have had.

The blogs I originally wrote to drive traffic to my website, of which the purpose was to market myself in my portfolio career. But that purpose also changed as the blogs took on a life of their own. I have written over 500 blogs covering a great variety of topics in over 700,000 words. By contrast *Threads and Patches* is mainly about me and family, friends and colleagues. I have decided to publish it anyway to mark my coming of age, i.e. my three score years and ten in 2020.

My idea was not to write a chronological tale but rather to develop themes – "threads" in computer speak – and to embellish them with "patches", which in computer speak means fixes or Band-Aids.

I have tried to balance the needs of privacy. Some things remain too private even for this limited audience. I have also not gone into a lot of detail about my career which I have covered elsewhere in a career summary written for my own benefit, but which can complement these notes. I have not disclosed all the problems, errors or other sadnesses that true biography ought to reveal. "Regrets, I've had a few, but then again too few to mention", as Paul Anka wrote for the immortal Sinatra to sing. That, too, is trite but the words seem to work.

September 2020

David Pearson

"I have measured out my life with coffee spoons."
After *The Love Song of J. Alfred Prufrock* – T.S. Eliot

I measured out my life by climbing trees,
By dabbing witch hazel on scraped knees,
And learning how to cook by toasting cheese.
I measured out my life by stealing kisses,
And chasing after a mix of missing misses,
Receiving on this stage both boos and hisses.
I measure out my life by hiking miles,
By climbing hills and climbing stiles,
And keeping records in my files.
I measure out my life by playing games,
By dropping catches and dropping names,
Recalling rare past glories (and forgetting shames).
I measure out my life by catching trains,
By learning how to live with aches and pains,
By slowly killing off the cells in brains.
I measure out my life by catching planes,
By getting stuck in both slow and fast lanes,
By fearing that the loss outweighs the gains.
I measure out my life by making cracks,
By missing meals and catching snacks,
And failing to avoid the weight of tax.
I measure out my life with coffee spoons,
By bopping to the best of Broadway tunes,
And greet a sequence of Blue Moons.
I measure out my life by baking bread,
By striving hard to be better read,
And spend at least eight hours per night in bed.

Introduction

I arrived on this earth in the middle of a century (1950), in the middle of a year (June), in the middle of a month (the 14th), in the middle of a week (Wednesday), a quarter of the way through the day (at 6 a.m.). I arrived in Brierley, a nursing home in Surrey. The country was over the euphoria of defeating the Nazis after six terrible years of struggle and waking up to the fact that there was a new enemy, Communism, facing the Western free nations, on much wider fronts. Mao Zedong had the year before established the Communist state of China and had started the Korean War just weeks before.

DP aged 7 months, 1951.

The country was also still paying the cost of war and of the excesses of an over-enthusiastic Socialist government which had spent money it did not have on nationalising great swathes of British industry. As a result the pound had fallen by 40 per cent against the dollar and many items of household goods were still rationed.

My parents had played their part in the fight against totalitarians and were to leave these new fights to others. My father, Eric, was now thirty and qualifying as a Chartered Quantity Surveyor. At Tiffin's School as a young man of sixteen he had suffered a rugby injury. This had cost him six weeks of valuable study and he was unable to catch up. So when a master read out a notice calling for applicants to E.R. Babbs & Sons, a firm of Quantity Surveyors with offices in Piccadilly, he responded to the call without the faintest idea of what a Quantity Surveyor actually did. He left school in 1936, the year of the abdication crisis. But Eric was sensitive to a greater growing crisis in Europe and was in that group of patriotic Englishmen who thought policies of appeasement followed by the then governments of Stanley Baldwin and Neville Chamberlain unwise. He was sure that a second war would have to be fought against the Germans and knew that he was ready to fight it. Six months before war was declared, he signed up for the Territorial Army. He was called up on 1st September 1939, two days before the declaration of war, and in 1940 joined the Royal Artillery.

He was the youngest son of James Pearson, a moderately prosperous horticulturalist and retailer with a shop in Malden. James' marriage to Rose was his second and he was in his fifties when Eric was born in 1920. Eric had three older brothers, Stanley, Leonard, and Bernard, and two older sisters, Vera and Phyllis, and Eric was inevitably spoilt as the youngest. The family were conservative and churchgoing and as a server, Eric was struck one day by the beauty of a young girl at her confirmation. Joan Esdaile Wyatt was the elder daughter of Jack Wyatt, a railway clerk, and Kathleen Minnie Wyatt, née Bell, who lived in Stoneleigh Avenue, in Worcester Park.

Jack, while hardly well paid, was responsible for the punctuality of Southern Railways. He did not need Mussolini to tell him how to get the railways to run on time. The railways were all still private companies; they had been so since their immensely successful foundation in the Victorian era. Jack would stand at the end of a platform at Waterloo station with his stopwatch. Should a driver bring in a train more than two minutes late he had to explain to Jack the reasons.

Joan was not only pretty but very bright, and won a scholarship to Sutton High School where she did well in the Humanities, particularly English Language and Literature, though she was less capable at the Sciences and Mathematics and was thus unwittingly a perfect foil for her future husband.

After the outbreak of the Second World War they became engaged and once it was clear that Eric's regiment was to be sent abroad they resolved to get married. The ceremony took place on 10th February 1942 and later they had a modest honeymoon at Bramley. Soon after, Eric was despatched to Madagascar. He was not to return until after the war against the Japanese was over. In Madagascar the fighting was light but in 1943 the regiment was sent to join Field Marshal Slim's XIV Army campaign in Burma, which was one of the most bitter in the whole war. Eric lost many of his colleagues but he himself was charmed and only felt a bullet pass close by. The bullet hit a tree and a resulting splinter scratched Eric's arm. It was the only physical injury he sustained but he suffered terrible mental effects with horrible nightmares continuing into old age.

On another occasion he was about to drive a jeep into the jungle when a superior officer – Eric was then a lieutenant – came up to requisition the vehicle and drove it off himself. Within seconds the vehicle was attacked by enemy fire and all its occupants killed instantly. Eric learnt that the officer's name was Eric Wyatt. My father's name was Eric and my mother's maiden name was Wyatt!

Dangerous though this undoubtedly was, Joan may have faced even greater danger. She spent her war years working for His Majesty's Stationery Office and volunteered as a Fire Watcher. She spent many nights on the roof of the office building watching for enemy bombers and incendiary bombs during the Blitz.

Eric and Joan wrote extensively to each other during these difficult years. It is perhaps hard for a modern reader to imagine how a young couple, still in their teens at the start of the war, could lose so much of the best years of their lives to this colossal war. When the war in Europe came to an end Joan found it difficult to celebrate with all her friends, as the war in Burma was still taking a terrible toll. Finally the bombs were dropped at Hiroshima and Nagasaki and the Japanese surrendered. But return was not immediate as there was still much to do in the aftermath of the war. Eric returned home to much rejoicing at the end of 1945, nearly four years after he had married and then left his bride.

They were together for only four weeks before he was called up again, this time to join the British Army of Occupation of the Rhine in Germany. The war there was over, but there was still much to do. It seemed most unfair, particularly as there were many who had fought only a short war by comparison, but little is fair once people go to war.

Once he was finally demobbed in September 1946 he resumed his career as a budding Quantity Surveyor with E.R. Babbs & Sons. He worked very hard taking his exams. The young couple lived first with Joan's parents then set up on their own. They moved frequently in those first few years after the war and Angela was born in August 1947. When she was two there was almost a major tragedy as she contracted meningitis and nearly died. Fortunately, she came through and enjoyed rude health from then on except for suffering chronic short sightedness.

I came on the scene in June 1950. Eric was doing well and in 1954 was asked to move to Manchester to set up a branch office. Today such a move sounds trivial but in those days with no motorways it was probably equivalent to the modern move abroad. Eric went to start his new role and find somewhere to live and the rest of us stayed with Len and Rene Pearson and our cousins Tim and Frankie. Len owned a shop in West Wickham selling pet foods and accessories and the family lived over it. It was an amusing diversion but in May 1954 shortly before my fourth birthday, we moved to 4, Elmsleigh Road, a semi-detached mock-Tudor house in Heald Green, a village in Cheshire close to Ringway (later Manchester) Airport.

Part I
Career

Connections

"Only connect."

Howard's End – E.M. Forster

As a student of History I rejected the various interpretations that sought to unify the explanations of historic developments in one great thesis. I particularly spurned the Marxist theory that placed some economic rationale at the foundation of history. If there was a single explanation, I argued it lay in the behaviour of people; but this was, of course, circular because the historian was trying to explain that behaviour.

Later, I became aware of Darwin and believe *On the Origin of Species* to be as important a work of history as there has ever been. The struggle to survive, the survival of the fittest, is the most powerful of motivations and explains much of what we call history.

But there is still much that is random in that process.

Some religions teach that it is all predetermined. One cannot prove this wrong but it seems to me a hopeless philosophy. If it is predetermined then I have no choice. If I have no choice what is the point of anything? It is by making choices that we show what we are.

So my life has consisted of a number of random events linked by either choice or accident. I believe you make your own destiny. But I also believe that random events can decide its course. Let us see.

As I have explained, on Boxing Day 1945 Eric was called back to his regiment to serve in post-war Germany. He was not to return until the summer of 1946. My sister Angela was born the following year and after further connections, presumably in September 1949, I arrived at 6 a.m. on the morning of Wednesday 14th June 1950. My father worked hard at his chosen profession of Quantity Surveying. He had lost seven crucial years from age 19 to 26 and tried to make up for lost time. He studied hard at night and qualified as a Chartered Surveyor.

There was only one local school that Angela and then I could attend and that was Gatley County Primary School. I have written in another thread ("Institutions") of my progress to Manchester Grammar School, promoted by my desire to play football and not rugby, and then my good fortune in winning a scholarship to America and a place at New College, Oxford University.

By the third year of Oxford I was faced with all the choices of a careers festival. My original plan to read and then practise Law had become stale and I realised that that as a career held few attractions for me now. It would be largely academic, I reasoned, in the sense that I would always have to spend time in the library keeping up to date. It would probably tie me to London, not a prospect for which I was ready.

I hunted around. I even went to Australia House and enquired about emigrating there. A friend of mine, Paul Wait, did just that and stayed there. I went on the milk round, interviews with a series of large companies recruiting in the major universities. I applied to oil companies and other conglomerates, and had follow-up interviews with several. At this time my efforts and my studies were interrupted by a bout of glandular fever. By the time I met Procter & Gamble, applying for a job as Sales Representative, I was a bit fed up with the whole process. Instead of wearing my ill-fitting suit, I wore my best George Best outfit, rust coloured sports jacket, green trousers and a blue shirt with a scarf. The interview went brilliantly.

When the interviewer, a charming professional, asked me, "Well, Mr Pearson, you have put down a lot of interests here. Which are the most important to you?"

I answered, "I didn't put down the most important – they would be booze and birds!"

He said, "Thank God! I am so fed up with interviewing people who claim to have some deep intellectual passion for the cinema. I want to scream at them, 'What do you do for fun?'"

Ever since, in every interview I have ever conducted, I have asked, "What do you do for fun?"

This is about connections and I was now connected to Procter & Gamble, possibly the leading company in the world in offering business training on the job. They were excellent throughout the process of recruitment and finally I was being interviewed for a real job by John Scott, District Manager, and John Procter [sic], Area Manager. They asked me if I was "mobile".

"Yes," I replied, "but I would not go to Northern Ireland."

"Oh! Why not?"

"Well, you could say political reasons.'"

"What are they?"

"Cowardice."

It was just as well. John's District included Northern Ireland. But they took me at my word and offered me a job starting in August 1971 in Yorkshire.

But it was conditional on a clean driving licence.

I did not have a driving licence. When I returned from my year in America, my father had started to teach me to drive when we were on a family holiday in Selsey, West Sussex, staying with his sister, Phyllis, and her husband, Dick. We went out on my first ever lesson in the Ford Corsair and when we returned it was to the news that my uncle Len, brother to my father and my Auntie Phil, and my godfather, had been killed in a road accident in Spain. He had been in the passenger seat of his car, driven by his daughter Frankie's boyfriend, Clive, when a coach came round a bend on the wrong side of the road and hit the car head on. Len was killed instantly; Frankie was badly injured although Clive walked away without a scratch.

This put me off driving and I went through my three years at Oxford cadging lifts or hitch-hiking, but avoiding driving myself. Now with Finals a few weeks away it was more important to pass my test than to gain my degree. I did both and started life as a trainee Sales Representative.

Years later I would joke that the only sensible thing to do with a Law degree from Oxford was to become a toothpaste salesman. Under pressure I would rationalise that only about half of those who take a Law degree go on to practise, and indeed many famous lawyers did not take a first degree in Law but changed later.

The truth was that my original thinking about Law as a degree was flawed. I had believed that a Law degree was in a way vocational, in contrast to a degree in the Arts like History, for which I might also have entered. In fact most Arts courses are, or certainly were, similar, in that they prepare for a wide range of careers.

Procter & Gamble kept its word, providing an exceptional quality of training on the job. Within two weeks I was conducting sales calls on my own. Within two months I was responsible for a territory of business. Within six months I was winning prizes in sales competitions. I had a flair for the work and enjoyed it. They certainly treated my mobility as part of the deal. I was moved all over Yorkshire with stints in Rotherham, Hull and Sheffield. There was a brief sortie in Wales, then an assignment in Manchester, which allowed me to live back at home for a while. During this period I started to conduct training: i.e. I was no longer being trained; I was training others. Eventually I trained more than twenty. The first was in Glasgow. Then I was head hunted within the company. This was a standard process by which another District Manager would appoint a new District Field Assistant (DFA). During this first part of my sales career I had already reported to several different managers and benefited from each one. Now I was appointed to work for Nick Heptonstall, an outstanding manager, who later formed his own successful consultancy. Nick's District was the old Anglia TV region though his office was in Coventry. I found a bed-sit in Ramsey in the middle of nowhere.

The job of DFA is the one trainee manager position in the company. Your job is to become a manager. In the process you will of course conduct lots of other tasks, but I wrote my own training programme. I was the first to do this. The other Area Managers, particularly an old salt called George Read, trained me.

I was ready to become an Area Manager but first I was asked to work on an exciting project, the national launch of Head & Shoulders shampoo and Crest toothpaste.

After extensive test marketing these two toiletry brands were finally going to be rolled out nationally. The key to the establishment of a brand is distribution. Much of this could be achieved by central negotiation but there were still thousands of independent grocers and chemists who would not normally receive a sales call from companies like P&G. Roy Franchi, our charismatic Sales Director, had decided that part of the launch programme should be the establishment of a commando sales team to sell the initial products direct from their cars. I was chosen to head up the southern team and a fellow DFA, Geoff Tagg, the northern team, and we both reported to a bright Area Manager called Bob McCulloch.

Fortunately for me, Bob had some leave, so I had the job of setting it up. By the time he returned I had already organised the whole affair, negotiating the packages with the Brand Managers and the administration with the Finance Dept. and developing the sales story.

I found a house to rent by Heathrow airport, right under Runway One flight path. An Oxford friend, Allan Leonard, and his sisters joined me and for the next six months I was on the road in my first quasi-management position. It was not full Area Management; the sales reps were not really my responsibility. At the end of the programme they would revert to their

Miss United Kingdom, sponsored by Camay. DP on right.

home districts. But it was a start. I was confident that I would soon have an area of my own.

That was to come with another company. Henry Jackson had been the star Area Manager displayed in the P&G recruitment programme to show what was possible. He had studied at Imperial College, London and had reached management in two and a half years. He was later recruited by Pedigree Petfoods, a division of Mars Ltd., and by now was its Thames Regional Manager. He called me at home to test my interest in joining their company as an Area Manager. It was my first experience of being head hunted and proves my thesis of connections. He had got my name from his former colleagues as an up-and-coming potential Area Manager.

The recruitment process was vigorous and challenging, involving group as well as individual interviews. I passed that and joined the company as Essex Area Manager in January 1976, on double my previous salary.

Pedigree was expanding and with it had expanded its sales force. Four new areas had been created but they were only able to fill one of these positions internally. Three of us were recruited from outside, two from P&G. My experience of training was a big factor in my favour. Over the next two years I had four of my own people promoted: Ernie Armstrong, Graeme Butt, Simon Gould and Jerry Fowden. All these men went on to do well, some with other companies. Jerry later became MD of Rank and Simon Sales Director of the importers of Bacardi.

I also met my targets and won several competitions. Henry had transferred to brand management and was succeeded briefly by John Eustace, also from P&G. John immediately stepped up to run the Southern Division and Malcolm Hewitt, a Geordie National Accounts Manager, took over. At a sales meeting set up by John with the Non-Canned Marketing Team I received a gift from Chris Bradshaw, the Marketing Manager, on behalf of the rest of the sales team. Later Chris was to recruit me to his team of Brand Managers.

I moved to Peterborough, where our semi-moist products were manufactured, and bought a thatched cottage in nearby Oakham.

At a sales conference early in my career with Mars one of the directors, Mike Pullin, started to talk to me at the bar. At the time it appeared spontaneous. I later surmised it had been planned. He told me that those who wanted to reach Zone III in the company, i.e. director level, should have experience of more than one discipline, more than one product category, and preferably more than one country. I was to gain all three.

In Mars, the convention was that you were free to apply for alternative roles in other parts of the group, and so in following Mike Pullin's advice I had applied for sales roles at Mars Confectionery but had not been successful. Now a telex was circulated advising us of an opening at KalKan, our Petfoods business based in Los Angeles. By now I had assumed responsibility for the company's export sales, as well as my brand management responsibilities. I was certainly qualified for the role and I applied. A small group selection was held near Heathrow with Mike Murphy, KalKan's VP of Personnel (and later President), and this time I was successful. I was invited to fly to Los Angeles for further interviews. I sought advice from our Pedigree Personnel Director, David Drennan, and he said I should not go with a typical laid-back English attitude of expecting them to sell the job to me. If I wanted the job I should go with a gung-ho attitude of what I was going to do for them. This advice proved sound and I was offered the role of International Marketing Manager at KalKan, responsible for all their sales outside the continental United States.

And so in May 1980 I emigrated from the UK with no idea of when I would return. I was single and had an expense account and the chance to travel the world first class on business. I bought a condominium in Culver City and set about my task. I visited Japan, Puerto Rico, Canada, Sweden, the Bahamas, Trinidad and Curaçao and developed business in all those countries. I also transacted with Bahrain, Taiwan and others without managing to visit.

But the most interesting was Chile. My colleague at M&M/Mars, Robert Ferrante, had started a candy business selling through an importer owned by Mario Selman Deik. He thought that Petfoods might be worth a try and invited me to accompany him on a trip to see the market. In August 1980 I visited Chile for the first time and fell in love with the country, its people and everything about it. Robert and I went back with John Coady, Development Group President of Mars Inc, in November. John's role was to develop new businesses in emerging markets. He asked us to go on a third visit in January 1981 with a member of the planning dept. to formalise a recommendation to start a marketing company there.

Threads and Patches

I had not thought who should run this. I just thought it was necessary to manage the opportunity better. But John asked me if I would do it and it seemed to realise my ambitions. John Barrow, President of KalKan, with whom up to this point I had barely exchanged words, now pressed me to reject the offer and stay with KalKan. He valued the work I was doing, particularly with sister companies. I was being fought over and it was a nice feeling.

I decided to move to Chile and start a marketing company, the first in South America. I reasoned that after this I would go to larger markets as they opened up and finally perhaps head up the whole region.

At KalKan, I was introduced to Bank of Boston as a bank who might help me in Chile. The bank was also expanding its operation in South America. I opened a personal account with them and then, in Chile, opened the Effem (Chile) Ltda. account there. No. 3 in the bank, recently arrived, was an American, James Callahan. We became friends and often played golf together. Jim was a fine golfer, very much better than me, but was patient and willing to put up with my hacking. On one occasion we played with two brothers, one by the name of Pancho.

DP in Maipo Valley near Santiago, Chile, June 1981.

At a party at the Callahans', I met Pancho and his wife Lucero; they had just had a baby, Kika, but the marriage was not to last. A few months later I was asked if I knew someone to go out with Lucero as she had split up from Pancho. I suggested another gringo friend, Rick McCreight, an advertising man down in Chile for an assignment with Grey Advertising. Rick and Lucero dated for a few months. They had their ups and downs but fortunately the relationship lasted long enough for Lucero to introduce me to her sister, Carmen, nicknamed Coca, recently returned from living in Spain.

Carmen (Coca)

This was July 1982 and things were starting to go badly in the Chilean economy. Our business had been built on shifting sands. The exchange rate had been fixed for three years, allowing importers to do very well. It was now devalued drastically and importing became very difficult, even impossible. (It was the seventh deepest depression in modern world history: Wall St 1929 was first; Soviet Union 1989 was second; Chile in the winter of 1982 was seventh.) In October 1982 I flew to Brazil to recommend to John Coady and Forrest Mars that we close Effem Chile. After a day of tough discussions they accepted my recommendation.

I flew on to Rio to meet John Eustace, a connection at P&G and Pedigree Petfoods, who by now was running his own food brokerage. He wanted me to join him, so if I could not continue my career with Mars I had an offer at Crombie Eustace. I flew back to Chile to effect the closure of Effem Chile

Ltda, which I completed in February 1983. But first I asked Coca to marry me. She said yes and we got married in December 1982. Whatever my experience had been in Chile from a business point of view, it had given me the most important connection of all, my wife.

Wedding Day, December 1982.

Institutions

"I would not join any club that would have me as a member."

Groucho Marx

I suppose the first club that I joined was the Church of England. They did not ask me but I am still a member. My godfathers Uncle Len and Uncle Bernard and my godmother "Auntie" Kath took vows on my behalf and I was confirmed at the age of 12. Despite many attempts I have never been excommunicated and, of course, like many others I still attend for baptisms, weddings and funerals. When my parents married, the local paper headline was "Two church people wed". I was brought up to know of no other way and attended Sunday School, then joined the choir, and when my voice broke I became a server. Much of my social life revolved around the church and my best friend in my teens, Neil Culliford, was the vicar's son.

I joined the Boy Scouts as a cub, learnt all the nonsense about "Dyb! Dyb! Dyb!" and became something of a badger as my father called it, in that I gained seven proficiency badges. More importantly it gave me my first formal experience of leadership when I became a sixer, i.e. the leader of a group of six. I did not move automatically into the Scouts, as I waited for a friend of mine, David Marsh, to join me at Manchester Grammar School and join one of their four troops. He reneged on this deal and I decided not to bother. Some years later I was invited to join the local Senior Scouts and quickly caught up all I had missed.

My schooling was steady and unspectacular. I attended Gatley County Primary School where I was usually top of the class. Then at the age of 9 I took the entrance exams for Manchester Grammar School (MGS) and William Hulme's, Manchester. I won places at both and selected MGS because it played football while William Hulme played rugby. My rugby-playing cousins, John and Nigel, went to William Hulme but I was a very small boy and could not imagine what physical harm would befall me if I tried. This happy selection had nothing to do with the fact that MGS was possibly the leading school in the country.

I was ten when I started and there were only two or three boys younger than me in the school. I started in 1 gamma, the third stream on the classical side, and believed that I could always repeat a year if necessary. At the end of a first year where I finished eighth in the form I suggested to Richard Harris, my form master, that I stay down a year. He countered that he had recommended me to go into II alpha, the top stream. I was able to maintain this, taking O-levels at fourteen and A-levels at sixteen, and tried out for Oxford at sixteen. Again, I did not expect to succeed and was prepared to repeat and try again the following year.

Amazingly I was successful and was accepted by New College to read Jurisprudence in 1968. I was competing against a generation they had not yet met and the free year had to be put to some other use. I had always wanted to visit America and had thought that if this opportunity should arise I would apply for an English Speaking Union scholarship. I then found out that such scholarships were far from free. I played with the romantic notion of working my passage but discovered that that was a thing of the past, having been outlawed by the Seamen's Union. My form master, Dr Denis Witcombe, came to my rescue with a leaflet for the American Field Service (AFS). I wrote to its director in Oxford, David Watson, who said that entries for that year were closed but in view of my exceptional situation, would I travel to Oxford for an interview? I found myself having my second interview in Oxford in a month and this was similarly successful.

In August 1967 I travelled to Minnesota by way of orientation at Loughborough University and Hofstra University in Long Island. I became a pupil of the Blake Country Day School for boys. This was a private school in a country where comprehensive education was already well established. This meant that I maintained a good educational standard. I was compelled to study English, as a foreign student, and History (of the US). In addition I took courses in Contemporary Civilisations (i.e. modern US history) and Comparative Religions. I came second in the class and graduated Summa Cum Laude.

But I had also joined the AFS. This was founded in the First World War as a volunteer ambulance service. It repeated this service in the Second World War and was then asked to help rehabilitate attitudes to German citizens by sponsoring the exchange of high school students. From six placements in 1946 it had grown by 1967 to 3,000 in the US and another 1,500 from the US to 60 countries.

DP in USA 1968

When I returned home I became a Returnee and as the organisation was based in Oxford I quickly became involved as a volunteer. After a few years of this involvement I was elected President of AFS (UK). I was just twenty-four and was responsible for recruiting the full-time Director of the Programme.

Also, when I returned, I went up to New College, Oxford University, two venerable institutions. My time there is the subject of other threads and patches but the friendships and loyalties made there have lasted as long as any I have made.

Those who work in sales and marketing like to think that they have a profession, but it is not a career run by professional bodies in the way that the law or accountancy is. These careers are protected by institutional bodies that set exams and limit the membership of their profession. They thus effectively run a closed shop.

Anyone can get into marketing and many do. There is a Chartered Institute of Marketing (CIM) that does set exams and has some 20,000 members. However, it has little credibility in setting minimum standards for the profession. I later became a Fellow of the CIM but did not have to take any exam to earn this honour. Of far greater credibility are those companies that have recruited and trained to their own high standards and I was fortunate enough to work for two of them, Procter & Gamble and Mars.

I did attend a course of the CIM when I transferred from sales to marketing in 1978. It was a week-long residential course and was reasonably well taught, but there was no question of passing anything, just attending. That same year I joined the Marketing Society for the first time, attracted by its conference line-up. Famous speakers included Roy Hattersley, who was then Canute-like trying to push back the tides of inflation by controlling prices and causing immense long-term damage to the economy as a result, and other business leaders of the day. Apart from my years abroad I have been a member ever since.

At Sony I became a more active member when I was asked to chair a sector of the membership for consumer electronics. I modelled it on the successful Fellows' Dinners. I was not yet a Fellow but had attended some and enjoyed the format. I ran a series of dinners, about three per year, well attended by members and their guests who were attracted by a top-name speaker from our industry, who was in turn attracted by my invitation as a senior figure in that industry. From retail we had Brent Wilkinson, then MD of Comet; John Clare, then CEO of Dixon's; Mike Metcalf, then CEO of Thorn; and Eddie Styring, Chairman of Comet. Particularly well received was Julian Richer of the eponymous Richer Sounds, with whom we became great friends. From manufacturing we had Barry Morgans, ex-MD of IBM, UK; Sir Alan Sugar, founder-CEO of Amstrad; and Sir James Dyson, founder-CEO of Dyson. From the service side we had the late Stafford Taylor, then CEO of Cellnet; Sir Christopher Gent, then CEO of Vodafone; the late Richard Dunn, then Executive Director of News Intl.; and David Docherty, Deputy Director of the BBC.

For these efforts, in 1995 I was invited to be a Fellow of the Marketing Society and I later became an Honorary Fellow. There are some 3,000 members of the Society but only a limited number of Fellows. The same year, I was elected to the UK Hall of Fame for Marketing. Sponsored by ITV, these awards were also organised by the Society. The previous winners were Sir Alistair Grant of Safeway, Sir Geoffrey Mulcahy of Kingfisher, Robin Whitbread of Sainsbury and Eric Nicoli, then of United

Biscuits and later EMI. Unfortunately the Society did not maintain a consistent approach to these awards and the so-called Hall of Fame was not continued. So to my knowledge there are only the five of us who have been so honoured.

A fellow Fellow of the Society, Peter Mitchell, proposed me for membership of another semi-exclusive group, The Marketing Group of Great Britain. This had been formed as a dining club in the 1950s and still existed for that purpose, with membership restricted to 150 drawn from the top of the profession and with a strict rule of limiting membership to one per company. Black Tie dinners were held at Claridge's with a strong tradition of attracting top speakers. Most recent Prime Ministers, all the leaders of the opposition and equivalent business leaders have addressed the group. I remained an active member for five years or so but resigned when I moved my offices to Huntingdon and found it more difficult to attend London dinners. I also had objected to the way in which bookings were managed. On one occasion Gordon Brown, then Chancellor of the Exchequer and probable Prime Minister in Waiting (actual as it turned out), was booked as the speaker. Some members immediately booked tables of ten and others were forced onto a waiting list. I was in the latter group and then was offered a place in a second room with a closed circuit TV relay. I found this objectionable.

David Pearson with Sue Farr, head of Marketing at the BBC, who is holding David's UK Hall of Fame Award.

A much better-organised group is the Worshipful Company of Marketors. When I was invited to join in 2003 I had not heard of this particular Livery company. The tradition of the Livery Companies in the City of London is a venerable one reaching back many centuries. Some of the older companies are based on the original guilds which managed long-died-out professions like mercers and cordwainers. For several centuries no new charters were issued until in the 20th century it was realised that there were many new professions which could benefit from a Livery company. Thus the Marketors (note that "o") came into being in 1975. It, of course, has none of the grandeur of the ancient Livery companies with their magnificent halls and their colossal endowments but it can hold its events at these same halls as the companies are all on mutually friendly terms. Its activities are not confined to just dinners, but are also educational, charitable and social in the broadest sense. My wife Coca and I enjoy the social events, which must always have a touch of exclusivity about them, i.e. not be such as would be open to the general public.

I joined as a Freeman in 2004, admitted at an event at the Mansion House, and then after a period was invited to be a Liveryman. This involved first becoming a Freeman of the City of London. This last is not an honour and not really restricted, being open to almost anyone who can pay the requisite fee, but has an aura of exclusivity, and mythology surrounds its supposed privilege. So while never belonging to a professional institution I have in fact found myself in the unique position of being the only person who has been a Fellow of the Marketing Society, a Fellow of the Chartered Institute of Marketing, a member of the Marketing Group of Great Britain, a Liveryman of the Worshipful Company of Marketors and elected to the UK Marketing Hall of Fame.

I was elected a Fellow of The Royal Society of Arts, Manufactures and Commerce in 1995. This society was founded in 1754 by William Shipley with the mission "To embolden enterprise; to enlarge science; to refine art; to improve our manufactures and to extend our commerce". It has played an important part in leading public opinion and policy in a non-partisan way with contributions such as The Great Exhibition of 1851; the Festival of Britain in 1951; The Royal Academy of Arts; and the Royal College of Music; and more recently in 1995 the Tomorrow's Company Inquiry. I became a Life Fellow in 2006.

I found my role in the Worshipful Company of Marketors developed. I originally joined it for social reasons. While I worked at Sony there was a very active corporate social life which both Coca and I enjoyed. We entertained our dealers at The Royal Opera House and Wimbledon; we even went on holiday with them to places like Boca Raton and Tahiti. But when I decided to work for British companies this all stopped. And so the Marketors filled the gap with great social occasions with like-minded people. But gradually I realised there was much more to it than that. The social life provided the glue but was not the purpose. Rather, that was about supporting the Civic City and the Mayoralty, and the profession of marketing, and giving back both in money and time.

I was asked to chair committees, then go on court, then was elected Junior Warden, which meant subject to election, I would eventually head the Company as Master for a year, in my case 2016. During my year I wrote many blogs about my experiences which in 2017 I published as a book called *Marketing for Good is Good Marketing*.

At the end of the year all the Masters of the various companies got together to form a Past Masters Association. As our year marked the 350th anniversary of The Great Fire of London we called ourselves the Phoenix Masters and our consorts called themselves the Firebirds. We, too, thought there should be more purpose than just socialising and I was asked to lead this effort as Chairman of the Outreach & Purpose Committee. We have helped the Lord Mayor's Appeal Office increase participation in City Giving Day and also helped them with Sir Charles Bowman's chosen charity, the Samaritans.

Coca and DP as Master Marketor.

Manners Makyth Man

"Manners makyth man."
William of Wykeham, Bishop of Winchester

New College, Oxford was founded in 1379 by William Wykeham, Bishop of Winchester. William was immensely powerful both as a politician and a church leader and enjoyed great riches from his position. He also founded Winchester College and there were many students who attended both.

It is not clear exactly why it was called New College. It was the seventh college to be founded in the University of Oxford and the second to be dedicated to St Mary; so one theory is that it was the New College of St Mary. It was also the first to be built on the quadrangle style that set the style for the rest of Oxford. It retained this talent for original thought and it is exemplified by the statue of Mary over the main gate, which shows her pregnant, expecting the Son of God.

The Dining Hall is reputed to be the oldest to have been in continuous use in the Western world. In this hall every night for three years we, as undergraduates, demonstrated perfectly our understanding of the founder's motto. We threw bread rolls, climbed over tables and no doubt exhibited many other disgusting qualities.

But we had fun, testing our wits on our bright contemporaries. The college had very distinguished Old Boys: Richard Crossman, Tony Benn etc. from politics; John Galsworthy, from literature; and many distinguished law lords, scientists and others of the great and good. In more recent times Hugh Grant, the actor, studied there and this was to be a boost to recruitment in time. Its academic staff stood comparison with any and in my time included Lord David Cecil, Freddie Ayer, Tony Quinton, and other less glamorous but equally talented stars.

In such an environment one had to succeed, if not academically then at least in the pursuit of self-improvement. Among my contemporaries were Gyles Brandreth, A.N. Wilson, and many others who went on to succeed in business, the law and other fields.

The first friend I made at the college was Peter Collman. I met Peter on the first evening, as he and I both looked at the notice board to see what were the plans to try out for football. Peter was a modest, unassuming man, but an excellent mathematician who played bridge to the highest standard. Highly companionable, he drove an old Rover and often ferried groups of us to pubs and football matches. He later enjoyed a successful career specialising in logistics management, where his formidable talent for logic was well deployed.

In trying out for football I made many other friends: Peter Morris, a chemist; Derek France, another mathematician; and Roger Phipps, a biochemist, all played in the first team that year with me. The captain, Dave Standley, was a good goalkeeper, and competing for reserve goalie were David Hughes and Stuart Millman.

David Pearson

I first met David Billington Hughes when watching the Mexico Olympics. Bob Braithwaite had just won Britain's first gold medal and Dave claimed to know his daughter. This aspect of Dave's character amused us over the years. He arrived in the world, so he said, in a police car in Crewe as they attempted to drive his mother to Wales so he could be born Welsh. By now his parents had migrated to Kirkcaldy in the kingdom of Fife and Dave had taken on many of the aspects of a natural born Scot. He had become a Celtic supporter and taught us the politically incorrect songs of the IRA. I celebrated a number of Hogmanays with him. Once the New Year arrived we would wander the streets first-footing. David claimed to know people at many addresses but they would let us in anyway and we would drink their whisky and move on. He was already bald and looked many years older. It was no doubt his appearance that attracted the *Observer* photographer who took an iconic picture of Dave, celebrating the end of Finals watched by Steve "Fingers" Miller. He later became a very successful teacher at Gordon Watson's in Edinburgh where he exercised his love of music and song by producing musicals.

The group of lawyers studying with me was particularly talented. Initially there were seven of us and our tutors were Patrick Atiyah, brother of Michael who was to become President of the Royal Society, and Tony Honoré, who went on to be Regius Professor of Civil Law at All Souls'. Gerald Barling, Charles Macdonald and David Rowell were our scholars and exhibitioners. All fulfilled their promise, took firsts and went on to successful careers at the bar. Gerald became particularly well known as an expert in European law and was knighted. David von Simson, Brampton Mundy and Jamie Dundas all went into banking. Jamie had a hugely successful career culminating as Chief Executive of the property company MEPC, where he made his fortune. Gerald, Charles, David,

David Hughes (on right) with Steve Miller.

Threads and Patches

Jamie and I were all featured years later in *People of Today*, not a bad ration for one year's intake.

We became eight when Allan Leonard decided to join us. He took his Moderations in History after one term, then realised that we took ours after two and that if he switched to Law could effectively have a full term off. I first met Allan when we both tried out for the college table tennis team. We both succeeded and eventually joined forces with Peter as the college third team. This was because Allan had discovered that there were two ladies' college teams competing in that division. We had a good record but it became necessary to lose to the ladies' teams to make sure that a) they were not relegated and b) we weren't promoted. Allan enjoyed this kind of games playing.

Allan's principal interest was in horse racing. If he could have taken a degree in it he would have got a first rather than the third he collected in Law. He claimed that his "uncle" was the great E.P. Taylor, breeder of Northern Dancer, sire of Nijinsky and many other great classic winners. Through this connection Allan became a member of the Robert Sangster syndicate and owned shares in The Minstrel, a Derby winner, and Alleged, which won the Prix de l'Arc de Triomphe.

Going to Paris in October to see the Arc became a regular jaunt. In the early days this was a desperate run in clapped-out cars, with no reserved accommodation and a frantic dash back for the overnight ferry after the race. Today thousands of trippers go from England in civilised comfort through the Channel Tunnel.

Allan's love of gambling took him to the City, where he first worked as a stockjobber and later as a commodity trader. He then set up his own commodity-trading business, Muirpace. Among his clients were the Thompsons and unfortunately, in covering up a lost position in their account, Allan committed a series of highly complex frauds. While not trying to enrich himself this was still foolish and certainly criminal. Allan paid his debt to society with a spell in jail but lost his marriage in the process.

The founder's motto, "Manners Makyth Man", has been much misunderstood. It was in fact a revolutionary thought for its time. He was saying that a man was defined by his behaviour rather than his breeding. In that respect New College certainly lived up to its motto. On arrival

I found I gravitated to those who had been educated at grammar schools. This was before these great institutions were destroyed by the Labour Party and while they were still educating outstanding children regardless of their breeding. Richer parents, it is true, sent their boys to the public boarding schools and initially there was something of a divide between us. The boys from the grammar schools all had regional accents. The public-school boys all spoke with the same received English. We dressed differently as well and, of course, we behaved differently because money is a differentiator.

However, this soon broke down. Certainly by the second year, I was choosing my friends for their personality not their background. Allan Leonard, educated at Cranleigh, was particularly instrumental in helping to break down these barriers. He and I merged our networks so that they became one. And that continued for a long time.

Part II

Happenings

A Cat Has Nine Lives

"I'm still here!"
Follies – Steven Sondheim

I have fallen from a bus and been hit by a bus. I have fallen down a mountain and fallen from a ski lift. I have skied into a tree and skied into a snowman. I have been hit by a fire engine and by a duchess. And like the words in the Stephen Sondheim song, "I'm still here".

As a boy I would fall and scrape or bruise my legs every day. I wore shorts until I was at least thirteen and I must have smelt of witch hazel all the time. I was hit in the face by a cricket ball, standing too close to the wicket. The following day I climbed Snowdon with my father with swollen lips and wounded pride.

Coming home from school I jumped off a bus to run for another. My head hit the road first and another lump was added to my oddly shaped bonce.

All of this was normal and I avoided breaking any bone in my body until I was thirty. That was because of skiing, with which I have had a special relationship.

The first time I came close to skiing was without skis and it almost ended in disaster. I trekked round Mont Blanc with the school in the summer of 1966. We carried all our kit with us on long walks and then pitched camp for a couple of days. From there we would go on "excursions", i.e. climb up the mountains without full kit. Descending from one of these we discovered a stretch of snow down which we could slide, standing up, quite well. And then a few of us found an even steeper slope and started to slide down. We were soon out of control and heading for a stone bridge at the bottom which would have cut any of us in two. Fortunately I reached out and crashed into one of my colleagues, knocking us both onto solid ground. One chap only got off the snow just before the bottom. This was a portent of what was to follow.

My American host "parents", the Hannahs, skied every spring in Aspen, Colorado. I was welcome to join them if I learnt first. So we had some painful lessons in less romantic Midwest resorts in places like Hardscrabble, Wisconsin.

By the time I reached Aspen I had achieved a respectable snowplough with the neighbours' skis. By the fourth day I had graduated to the Intermediate slopes. I was tracking an accomplished lady skier. I accelerated to pass a ski school stretched across the hill. Suddenly the lady in front of me stopped. I hadn't mastered this part and was faced with three choices. I could go straight on and hit her. I rejected this option. I could go below and accelerate even more. I rejected this one too. So I tried to go back up hill and found myself heading for the trees. My right ski passed neatly between two youthful trees right up to the boot where it snapped off. Amazingly I was fine but again my pride was deeply scarred. I had to wade down the mountain in four feet of snow.

I did not strap on a ski again for thirteen years until I was back in the Rockies with an AFS friend, Jeanette, who was a keen cross-country skier. I was amazed how fast I could go and was soon speeding along Sun Valley, Idaho. Then I saw a snowman. I decided to charge it, as a knight would joust with his lance. I stabbed it with my ski pole only to find that the snowman was an iceman. At first I thought my hand was just bruised but nine days later it was still black and blue. I took it to the office nurse who took one look and said it was broken. This was confirmed in an X-ray. The break was in the joint of my little finger and so I could move it. I wore it in a splint for two months and, as it was my right hand, needed to have my left-handed signature notarised so that my cheques would be honoured.

Later that year I had migrated to Chile where the skiing is also said to be good. I visited Farellones with friends and was persuaded to try my hand once more. They had the kind of ski lifts that work on the inertia principle and pull you along the ground. Unfortunately my reel paid out but did not pull back in and I found myself falling some thirty feet down the mountain. That was the end of my skiing career.

I have already described falling off a bus. Later, while walking in Oxford, I was hit by one in the Cornmarket. It was just a glancing blow but it was a good warming-up for the fire engine. Allan Leonard had just passed his test and had a brand-new company BMW. He and I were going on a golfing holiday with Peter Collman and Julian Williams. The night before, we were going out for dinner. Allan, as a novice driver, somewhat tentatively, but correctly, drove through green lights in Ruislip. As we crossed the junction we were hit square on from the left. Allan wrestled with the car and it hit railings at the angle of the crossroads. We had been hit by a fire engine that went at full speed through the red lights. Sitting behind me in the back was Ann, the girlfriend and later wife of Jack, Allan's brother. She and I took the brunt of the collision and went to hospital. My X-ray showed nothing but bruised ribs but Ann had broken her pelvis. It turned out that the fire engine was going to a hoax call, and that the driver had done this before.

But my most memorable encounter on the Queen's high road was in Derbyshire. I was looking for a place to stop for lunch. Ahead I saw a pub on the right just after a left-hand bend. I signalled and was in the act of turning when I was hit hard on the right side of the car. From almost no speed I had to brake sharply to stop the car from crashing into the dry stone wall. The door was stove in right along my arm but I was unharmed. I got out on the passenger's side and saw a large black Citroen stopped over 100 yards down the road. The driver, a lady, was leaning against the car. I got an accident report form and a clipboard and walked down to see if she was all right.

"That was the most stupid piece of driving I ever saw," she said. "Fancy turning right after a blind corner like that."

"If you think that was blind I hate to think what speed you were doing. Anyway, are you all right?" I inquired, ever the gentleman.

"I'm OK, but the wheel is a bit damaged."

"Well, if we are both OK I think it just requires that we exchange names and addresses."

So she wrote, "The Duchess of Devonshire, Chatsworth."

Immediately, I replied, "Oh! And I'm Mickey Mouse!"

And then I remembered where I was; Chatsworth was the next village. This was the Duchess. One of the Mitford girls. Her sister had been an admirer of Adolf Hitler. I walked back to the pub. Now I needed a drink.

"Are you all right?" asked the barman.

"I'm fine," I said, "just a bit shaken up."

"She's always doing that!" said the barman.

The Dentist's Chair

"I am escaped with the skin of my teeth."
The Book of Job 19:20

It is a cliché to fear the drill of the dentist but I have had good cause. My earliest and worst memories are of some man inflicting inhuman torture on my mouth. The English have small heads and large teeth. Their mouths are ill fitted to accommodate all these teeth and the rites of passage are not completed without the sacrifice to the gods of several teeth. The Americans spend small fortunes to straighten out this inheritance but being born with very large mouths assists them. This is necessary to fit in the huge quantities of food they require.

At about the age of 8 or 9 I was playing football after school when I remembered that I had to go to the dentist. I arrived late but they went ahead with my appointment and drilled various holes and filled them with that mercury compound that then proceeds to drip one of the most poisonous substances known to man into your system for the rest of your life. Wounded I staggered to the bus stop only to find that I had forgotten my money. I walked home in the dark, a journey of about two miles.

By fourteen, the crowding of teeth in my mouth had become acute. This required hospital treatment and this particular joy was enhanced by becoming a guinea pig for the students to study. A gaggle of them queued up to put their nicotine-stained fingers inside my mouth. A brace was fitted but I could not cope with this and I rejected it.

Years later, at thirty-one, I needed my wisdom teeth to be extracted. The Chilean dentist did this with local anaesthetic and managed to leave the stub of one in the gum. He drilled a hole in this, put in a bolt and proceeded to tug at this, placing his feet against the chair for support. It was the classic scene from the Hollywood cartoon, but it was not funny. I dripped blood in bed for two days.

More recently I was recommended to another hospital for a further round of treatment. Just one session reminded me of the scene in *Dirty Harry* where the psychopath pays a thug to beat him up to frame Clint Eastwood. Again teeth were removed and I was sent home to heal. But I didn't and the blood oozed out. In the middle of the night my wife called an ambulance and I was taken first to one hospital and then another, where it was sewn up. I spent the day in a ward where one man was having a new ear fitted, a second had eighty-three stitches in his leg and a third was interviewed by the police after a knife attack.

Namesakes

"A rose by any other name would smell as sweet."
Romeo and Juliet – William Shakespeare

The other day my cousin Frankie called.
"Hello?" I said.
"Frankie."
"Hello."
"Have you just won a coffee machine on TV?"
"No, why?"
"Well, I was watching TV and someone called David Pearson from Hertfordshire has won a coffee machine."
"There are an awful lot of us."
And there are.
I was born in June 1950 when David was the second most popular boy's name after John. Charles had been the name of the first son of Princess Elizabeth and Price Philip, although in my case it was a family name; my father was called Eric Charles, and his father was James Charles. Pearson is not quite as common as Smith, Brown and Robinson but not far behind. In the Manchester telephone directory there were pages of Pearsons and a good number must have had the Christian name David.

Pearson means Son of Peter, Peter's son, and so is synonymous with Peterson, Pierson, Peters, Pearce, Pierce, Pirsson, Perez, Petrov, Petrenko, McPherson, Fitzpiers, and no doubt many others. Peter of course was The Rock on which Jesus founded his Church and so the name Peter, Pierre, Pedro etc. is synonymous with rocks, stone etc.

My name became the source of many nicknames at school. Pearson was reduced to Pears, and play was made on my initials: D.C. became Deece, Deester and even Deestinks. Happily this last was very brief. More imaginatively, I attended a scout camp with a school troop where everyone was given a nickname, usually of cryptic origin; a friend, David Killion, became Samson (Kill-Lion), while more obscurely Tony Drake became Yapp (Francis Drake > Francis Yapp, a former teacher at the school). I became Pip (Pearson > son of a pear > little pear > a pip). But the nickname that stuck was Pancho. This derived from my support of Manchester United as there was a contemporaneous player called Mark Pearson who sported long sideburns and so was known as Pancho. This has survived to this day with some old friends. At my US school it was my Englishness that defined the nickname, so England, Limey etc. were all used. I picked up something of a trans-Atlantic accent there and so when I went up to University I was initially named Lester after the Canadian Prime Minister, Lester Pearson.

I first became aware of a namesake when I began to read the evening newspaper regularly. One day David Pearson, aged 17, was killed on his motorcycle. This gave me a strange feeling. Some weeks later David Pearson, aged 27, was married. Had this been a Resurrection? I realised that there were a number of us.

In 1967 I went to Minnesota on the AFS Exchange Scholarship. At Blake School I became aware that the previous year there had been a senior called David Pierson. That was OK but he had been the outstanding athlete in the school. He won colours in football, hockey and athletics, where he was co-captain. I immediately felt under pressure that I had to live up to Dave's reputation in some way. Fortunately I did, in soccer at least, where our team won the State Championship and I won Most Valuable Player Award. My friend Gregg Peterson, who captained the team in which we both won All-Conference Honours, still calls me All-England and himself All-State!

While I studied in America I was taught the importance of names. This essay complains about the problems of a common name but I learnt that those with distinctive names can suffer much more. Apparently there was a much-married socialite who finished up with the moniker Phoebc B. Peabody Beebe. Say it quickly and it sounds like a machine gun. Sadly, she took her own life. Another playboy had been christened William Newton Hooton. The American pronunciation of this is especially brutal and he finished in a lunatic asylum. Other strange but true names from American sources can be found in the following list:

Spiro Agnew	Armand Hammer
Oscar Asparagus	Learned Hand
Magdalena Babblejack	Ima Hogg
Olga Beanblossom	Mona Lisa Gooseberry
Wilburn Beerwart	Moon Landrieu
Spring Belch	Daisy Lobster
Sibyl Bibble	Dewy Odor
Fletcher Boogher	Ethel Oink
Ace Case	Lamoine Plopper
Aphrodite Chuckass	Faith Popcorn
Sinbad Condeluci	Elihu Root
Jubal Early	Moon Unit and Dweezil Zappa
Tony Fiasco	Clara Belle Sweat
Felix Frankfurter	Joe Terror

In business I started to deal with agencies of various kinds and again my reputation appeared to go before me. There was another David Pearson. I never met him but we corresponded and he ran his own advertising agency. He could have called it by some esoteric name but such is the power that he hit on David Pearson Advertising. I cherish a letter he wrote to me enclosing some blank letterheads with the caption: "Have fun with this!"

When I met my wife and gave her my name, far from giving her a common name I made her even more unique. She was already Carmen Libera Angela Veronica Chellew Bello. She now became Carmen Libera Angela Veronica Chellew Bello de Pearson. So distinctive was this that one Valentine's Day I bought her a star and named it after her.

Threads and Patches

When I joined Sony, the Japanese never came to terms with my name. It may appear common to Western eyes but to the Japanese they called me Pearson, Person, Parson even Peason.

And that reminded me of the immortal molesworth. This is actual dialogue from the lunch table between molesworth and his grateful friend peason:

"I think aldous huxley is rather off form in counterpoint, peason." And he replied, "I simply couldn't agree with you more rat face but peason is very 4th rate and have not got beyond bulldog drummond."

I was once booked on a return flight from Los Angeles with Virgin Atlantic. The flight was overbooked and there was considerable delay in issuing my boarding card. Many passengers were milling around and as we got closer to take-off time I became increasingly nervous. I asked for my boarding card on several occasions and was told it was not ready yet. Finally, with just a few minutes to go, I went up one more time and this time it was given to me. I got on the plane and with a sigh of relief settled down for the long overnight flight. Suddenly a man appeared claiming that I was sitting in his seat. He also had a boarding card with the same seat number and worse, had the same name, David Pearson. I had been issued with his boarding card. Fortunately the airline offered incentives for passengers to delay their flight to the following day. I could not delay as I had a Board meeting to attend. This man and his wife decided to accept the offer and so I was free to fly. I don't know what would have happened otherwise.

I have mentioned my wife's extensive names. Her patronymic, Chellew, is a Cornish name and the diaspora of Chellews from Cornwall in the 19th century to look for alternative mining work in the New World when the tin mines failed is a fascinating story. In researching it, Coca visited the Library of the Church of the Latter Day Saints in South Kensington. The Mormons believe that they can enlist the souls of the dead and so have an enormous archive of family records. Coca was researching her family and I met her there one day after work. I had a little time to kill and so I discreetly looked up my own record.

There it was on the slide. In the quarter April to June 1950, David Charles Pearson was one of FOURTEEN David Pearsons whose births were registered in England and Wales.

More recently, in August 2005, I set up my own company, DCP Associates Ltd. On receiving confirmations I checked how many directors of registered companies shared my name. I stopped counting at 200 and eight of those have Charles as their middle name.

I Was There (or Thereabouts)

> "It has been a damned serious business – Blücher and I lost 30,000 men. It has been a damned nice thing – the nearest run thing you ever saw in your life … By God! I don't think it would have done if I had not been there."
>
> Duke of Wellington

There is a Woody Allen film in which a character called Zelig, through the use of amazing special effects, appears to have participated in many of the great moments in history. The film *Forrest Gump* uses the same thesis and Tom Hanks is seen to shake Lyndon B Johnson's hand after the President has pinned a medal on him.

These films play to something in our psychology, the idea that we need to witness major events. The amazing scenes to celebrate the Queen's Golden and Diamond Jubilees are linked to this, that by being present, we somehow participate in the major defining events in our lives.

This is a stronger feeling than simply witness; I have seen many major sporting and theatrical events and so feel closer to those events than simply watching them on TV. After all, in supporting my team have not I somehow helped them to their victory? We know that the great musicians will respond to encouragement from the audience. But the idea of being directly involved, or closer to the action, is very powerful and I have felt it on a few occasions.

Threads and Patches

All of us remember where we were when we first heard of the death of President Kennedy or John Lennon, or more recently the terrible terrorist attacks on the World Trade Center and the Pentagon. I was at church when I first heard about the death of John F. Kennedy. I was living in the US when the news came in about Lennon's murder, driving back to my condominium after taking some Mars colleagues from Scandinavia out for dinner. I was running a sales conference for NXT when the news came again from New York, but this time about thousands of murders. Four of the attendees were American and all were frantically on their mobile phones to learn more and find out if they would be able to get home. I quickly brought the conference to an end and went straight home to join the world in watching the events unfold on TV. I learnt that I had been closer to this than I really wanted. One of the planes had been an American Airlines flight from Boston to Los Angeles. I had been on a similar flight just three weeks before after seeing my family on a flight home after a holiday in Cape Cod and Martha's Vineyard. This is as close as we want to get to events like this.

These tragic events seem to be happening all the time but the world's love–hate relationship with America brings their events to a heightened level. I was also living in the United States as an exchange student when both Martin Luther King and Senator Robert F. Kennedy were shot dead. I was a member of the school Glee Club and in the spring of 1968 we went on a tour to perform at various schools. The last concert was at a girls' school in Kansas City, Missouri. After the concert we enjoyed a mixer with the girls, and then the news of King's murder came in. The mixer broke up immediately and we left in our bus. Riots had already broken out all over the southern states. We were just 400 miles away from Memphis, Tennessee where the assassination took place. Our bus was shot at and we were ordered to lie on the floor of the bus. When we got back to our motel we were instructed to go straight to bed and not venture out onto our balconies. The following morning we returned to the relative safety of Minneapolis.

Just a few months later we had our school Prom at a local country club. All of us were on parade in our hired tuxedos and our dates looking their best in ball gowns. Proms go on through the night and so we were all awake when the news came from Los Angeles of the assassination of Bobby Kennedy. That killed any sense of celebration and we just sat around talking about the loss of innocence.

In 1980 I started to visit Chile for the first time and then the following year I was asked to go there and form a marketing company for the Mars Corporation. This was the era of Pinochet. He had come to power in 1973 in a military and violent *coup d'état*. Tony Hallett, a senior executive at Pedigree Petfoods where I had started my Mars career, on learning of my appointment, told me that my first hiring should be a bodyguard; such was the impression of South America. Actually I felt very safe in Chile. Yes, it was a police state and no one can defend some of the worst atrocities by the Pinochet regime in their first few years of power. But by 1981 it was a very pleasant place to live. Pinochet had just won a further eight years of power in a referendum and would then hand over to a democratically elected President. With tragic irony Tony Hallett was to die a violent death in a car accident in Norfolk.

One of my first hires was an Argentinean sales manager, Alberto Gentile. In the following spring Alberto asked me, "Don David, is there anything in the English papers about Las Malvinas?" He knew I kept up with the British newspapers. I received a weekly *Guardian* summary and also the *Sunday Times*, but there was nothing about the Falklands at that time. Apparently the Buenos Aires papers were already writing of an invasion. Of course the invasion happened and then the task force embarked on their eternal voyage, allowing time for Alexander Haig to attempt his shuttle diplomacy. But it also allowed time for Britain's secret forces to get into position, and that was in Chile.

I used to drink in the Sheraton Hotel with a friend, Rick McCreight, and one evening we fell in with some Brits who were very vague about what they were down there for! I guessed they were SAS. During the war itself I became very popular with the Chileans, as did all the British expatriates, because the Chileans had a long-standing enmity with their neighbours. One night in Viña del Mar I went to a bar with my Marketing Manager, Ramiro Berrios, and once it was known I was English I was treated as a hero and the folk group played all the English songs they knew.

All of this should have been history when the Metropolitan Police arrested an 82-year-old man in the middle of the night. He was heavily sedated and recovering from dangerous back surgery in a London clinic.

He was Augusto Pinochet. Now a senator, he was visiting London for both personal and business reasons. He had been received as a VIP. The then ambassador had spent years in exile and was no supporter of Pinochet but now had to handle the appalling diplomatic crisis that Jack Straw, to whom the Metropolitan Police reported directly, had created. Straw had visited Chile in his revolutionary youth and no doubt saw this as a way to redress the balance of history.

Coca, through her association with Las Señoras Chilenas de Londres, had regular contact with the ambassador's wife and we found out much more than was generally known. We attended a lecture given by Lord Lamont at the House of Lords and sat with him at table at a function of the Anglo-Chilean Society. No doubt there was a case for Pinochet to answer, but if so it should have been in his own country and not in Spain, which had its own appalling history and had never taken any action against any of Franco's terrible crimes.

In September 1984 I began working for Pillsbury, based in Hove. A few weeks after I started I was holding a planning meeting with my new marketing team at a hotel outside Brighton. That day the IRA attempted to assassinate the British Cabinet who were all staying at the Grand Hotel, Brighton for the Conservative Party Conference.

In 1987 I was on the last train out of London before the hurricane that Michael Fish failed to forecast closed down the tunnels between Victoria and Brighton, and then later that year I passed through Kings Cross just thirty minutes before the terrible fire.

I was approached to join a group of marketing experts to advise the Prince of Wales. He wanted to demonstrate to his tenant farmers in the Duchy of Cornwall that improved marketing would enhance their operations. He wanted this to help with the balance of payments in food. He wanted to encourage organic farming. And if there was a surplus he wanted this to go to his charities. All of these objectives were met through the successful launch of Duchy Originals. The first products were biscuits, then drinks, and now there are a wide variety of excellent products commanding a significant premium. For a number of years, I had the pleasure of meeting Prince Charles over lunch or tea at his homes in Highgrove or St James' Palace, or at other royal palaces like Sandringham.

On one occasion we were all invited with partners to a Christmas party at Kensington Palace. Both Charles and Diana used this occasion to thank the many people who had contributed their time to the many causes to which the two gave patronage. That very afternoon the Prime Minister, John Major, announced in the House of Commons that Charles and Diana would separate. We checked. The party was to go on. We turned up and stood in a long receiving line. Coca did her much-practised curtsey. Charles was charming. Diana looked terrible. Later Charles bumped into Coca and complained that he had not met her earlier. She complained that that was unfair, as she had been practising her curtsey for days.

Diana died in August 1997 and the nation watched the rather strange funeral. Blair gave his appalling impression of an archbishop reading from the bible. Shortly after, I was hosting a party of Sony dealers at our factory in Alsace and for entertainment after the dinner we had booked Ian Botham and Rory Bremner. Bremner gave a fabulous performance and afterwards over a whisky I asked him why he did not do an impression of Tony Blair. He said, "He's not funny." I said I thought he was hilarious and cited the performance at Westminster Abbey. Immediately Bremner did an uncanny imitation of Blair and soon after, this was a regular feature in his TV show. Indeed it became almost the only point of effective opposition to Blair.

I had the chance to meet Blair later that year. I received an invitation to a reception at Number 10. Coca and I arrived at the same time as the Japanese ambassador, Mr Hayashi, whom I knew well. He asked me, "Pearson-san. What is the purpose of this function?" I had no idea. The Japanese embassy had called the Foreign Office; but the Foreign Office could not enlighten them. Thus the representative of the emperor of our second-largest trading partner was invited to the official residence of the head of government and did not know the purpose of the visit.

That evening Blair was detained in the House of Commons as he was in the process of taking away allowances from single mums. Cherie therefore received the guests on her own. The attendance was decidedly mixed. There were business leaders and ambassadors. There were celebrities and charity workers. There were people who just looked ill. Chris Smith, the then Secretary of State for Culture, Media and Sport, came over and asked me if I wanted to buy an Opera House.

Threads and Patches

Finally the great man arrived and we then found out the purpose of the evening. It was to be photographed with celebrities like Chris Evans and with people in wheelchairs. These photos of course appeared in the tabloids the following day. We had another function to go to and so I went up to the Prime Minister to introduce myself. "Good evening, Prime Minister", I said. "I am David Pearson, Managing Director of Sony United Kingdom. Thank you for the invitation." Tony Blair replied, "It's a bit of alright this, innit?" The accent was Estuary and I, for once, was lost for words. Then Coca came up to be introduced and detecting her accent he asked her where she came from. "From Chile," she replied. "Oh, I'd love to go to South America. I never get to go anywhere interesting. I only get to go to Brussels." Again I was lost for words and Blair moved on to work the room. Since then he's certainly made up for lost time in visiting parts of the world more interesting than Brussels.

These few cases of involvement in major events are probably just examples of what the mathematicians call "Small World Syndrome". This is the theory that in just a few links one can connect any individual with any other individual. It is a small world!

Travelling

"To travel hopefully is a better thing than to arrive,
and the true success is to labour."

Robert Louis Stevenson

"Thomas Cook's first package tour in 1841 took 600 people where?" asked the quiz question. We speculated over the breakfast table. Florence? Venice? Paris? But no, it was that jewel of the East Midlands – Loughborough. Growing up in the 1950s, it was the convention to take a family holiday for two weeks in the summer at the seaside. Usually we drove to guest houses or small hotels in North Wales or the English South West. A favourite was Minehead in Somerset, which we visited three times. This was before the motorways had been built and so we had to break the journey and would stay overnight somewhere like Tewkesbury. We knew very few people who travelled abroad, and indeed, with exchange restrictions limiting an individual to £50, it would have been very difficult even if we had had the money.

My father had been abroad for most of the war years, carrying a gun rather than a passport, to Madagascar, India, Burma and finally Germany as part of the post-war occupation forces. My mother had never been abroad and only took her first overseas trip, for just a day, to Rotterdam with a Ladies' Group in the 1960s.

My father must have been doing quite well in his business in 1961 because we flew to Guernsey for a holiday in L'Ancresse. This was quite exotic, although my clearest memories are of staying in a darkened TV room to watch Richie Benaud bowl the Aussies to victory at Old Trafford.

Threads and Patches

My first trip abroad was with the school to France, Switzerland and Italy. Foreign Trek that year circumnavigated Mont Blanc in a clockwise direction. It was the summer of 1966, better remembered by most Englishmen as the year we won the World Cup. We were not even able to hear it on the radio, stuck up on a mountainside in Switzerland.

A year later I made my second trip abroad, this time as an exchange student to the USA. We met first for orientation at Loughborough University, without the help of Thomas Cook, and then flew by Air France to JFK. After further orientation at Hofstra University in Long Island, I took a bus through the night to Minnesota where I was to spend a year with the Hannahs. With them I took a skiing holiday in Aspen Colorado; with the school took a weekend trip to Chicago to see the Picasso exhibition; and also, with the Glee Club, toured Iowa, Oklahoma and Missouri to give a series of concerts. At the end of a marvellous year, 3,000 AFS students took bus trips around the USA to meet up in Washington DC. Our bus #30 followed an itinerary through Keokuk, Iowa; Springfield, Illinois; Lima, Ohio; Cattaraugus, New York; Barre, Vermont; Westchester, Connecticut; and Silver Springs, Maryland, our final base for the reunion in Washington DC. We were then divided into different groups and I stayed in one more community at Bethlehem, Pennsylvania, before boarding the SS *Waterman* in New York to sail home to Southampton.

Today's youth see taking a gap year between school and University as normal but my experience was most unusual for the age and made a significant impression on me. It gave me a taste for travel that I was never to fully satiate and probably influenced several of my subsequent career and life choices.

But the year had been heavily subsidised by the generosity of communities, schools and particularly host families. It had been the cheapest year of my education for my father to finance. As a student my ambitions had to be restrained.

In my first summer at Oxford I teamed up with two fellow undergrads, Peter Morris and Paul Wait, to go on a camping trip to Vienna, Venice and Zurich. Our plan was to take trains to Vienna and from Zurich, but to hitch-hike on all the intervening journeys. After a pleasant few days in Vienna we set out to hitch-hike south to Venice. After sticking our thumbs out for a whole day we gave up and returned to the same campsite. By now it was clear that we had severely underestimated the cost of this expedition and had to ration ourselves on everything. We took the train to Zurich, missing out Venice, and settled down in a campsite there for the second half of our trip.

I now realised that I could join a reunion of my AFS friends from bus #30 the previous summer. This was planned to be held in Strasbourg and I figured I could hitch-hike there in a day. My sister, Angela, had sewed together a Union Flag for me to pin to my bag as a way of picking up lifts. Armed with this I set off first for Basle and then Strasbourg. I started off all right and on the way out of Basle my flag did the trick. An Italian lorry driver picked me up to practise his English. However, he needed a lot more practice because he dropped me off too soon and I tried to hitch back onto the motorway. Eight hours later I had to give up and hitched a lift into the nearest town, Freiburg. I was now in Germany and had no local currency. I changed one pound at the railway station, bought a ticket to Strasbourg and while waiting for the train, decided to have a meal in the station restaurant. Knowing little German, I ordered "*Erbensuppe mit bochwurst*" to start with. A huge bowl of potato soup with four large sausages arrived. I ate three dishes worth and finally surrendered. I still had some change and bought a newspaper and bananas. Arriving late in Strasbourg I could not reach the hostel, which would be closed, and finally slept on a bench in a synagogue yard. It started to rain so I covered myself with the newspaper and slept under the bench. I arrived early at the hostel and woke up my AFS friends.

AFS gave me some other early opportunities to travel abroad: as a chaperone for the returning US students to their end-of-year gathering in Arnhem; and then as the AFS UK President with our full-time secretary to the European Conference in Birgitz, near Innsbruck in Austria. We flew to Munich only days after the Israeli Olympic athletes had been murdered and there was now a huge security presence everywhere with tanks on the airport runway. A case of closing the stable door …

Business travel began in a similarly modest way with Pedigree Petfoods when together with my brand management colleagues I took responsibility for some of the European markets. With our export manager I visited Belgium and Holland, my first overseas sales calls. Not long after, I was invited to apply for the role of International Marketing Manager for

Threads and Patches

KalKan in Los Angeles. I flew first class to Los Angeles, my first experience of this way of travelling. I checked in to the hotel and rang Mike Murphy, the head of personnel, who told me to get some rest and then he would take me out for dinner. With an eight-hour time difference I found myself dining and drinking cognac at what was effectively 5 a.m., but realised that Mike was testing my ability to deal with jet lag.

The job was to sell the company's products anywhere in the world outside the continental United States. There was some business in Puerto Rico and Japan and some enquiries from other parts of the world. I was single and had the chance to live in Tinsel Town and travel the world.

In the next year I visited Japan, stopping in Hawaii on the way back, Mexico, Canada, the Bahamas, Puerto Rico and other islands in the Caribbean, including Trinidad and Curaçao. In addition I got to know the USA very well including Los Angeles, New York, St Louis and San Francisco. I returned to Europe and, as well as visits back to the UK, visited France and Switzerland again and Sweden for the first time.

But most of all I visited Chile. I went there for the first time in August 1980, again in November for the FISA, in January 1981 to put together a plan to set up a marketing company, and then in March to start the process, and finally in May to head up that company.

While in Chile I travelled up and down that long, thin country, seeing more of it than most of its natives. I went to the far north, Arica, some

Torres del Paine, Chile.

19 degrees south, and the far south, Punta Arenas, 58 degrees south. If placed in the northern hemisphere it would stretch from Vancouver to the Baja California or from Edinburgh to Nigeria.

On one trip to the south to see various markets we flew commercially to Concepçion to meet Emilio Sandoval Po, our distributor. We then flew in his private plane down to the southern towns of Osorno, Valdivia and Puerto Montt. We stayed overnight in a hotel and then flew back. This time Emilio had his girlfriend with us. I was sitting in the co-pilot's seat. He told me to keep the plane level and pointing north and then moved into the back to canoodle with his girlfriend.

For the first time in my life I was flying a plane. My lesson had lasted about a minute. After the initial shock I found it exhilarating and, of course, very safe, as there were no other planes in that empty sky.

I took a private holiday to Easter Island, Tahiti, Moorea and Bora Bora. Easter Island should be a fascinating place to visit but I was so tired I overslept and missed the tour on the first morning. We were stuck on the island for three days and there were no other tours organised. There was no public transport of any kind. A hotel employee offered me the use of his motorbike, an incredibly generous gesture. I climbed on the bike and realised that I had no idea how to make it start let alone ride it, and in a state of considerable confusion dismounted. I did not really make the best of my trip to Easter Island and was therefore glad when the twice-weekly plane arrived.

But then the border police seemed to find a problem with my papers. In some countries this might be a cue for a bribe but not in Chile. I was mortified at the prospect of spending another four days on this bleak rock. Fortunately it was resolved and I flew to the much more exotic and beautiful islands of Tahiti.

I have written about my experiences in Chile during the Falklands War before (cf. "I Was There") but during that period I also went to Spain on a business trip. Our Spanish company had a factory in Vigo and so I flew up there to see it. On the way back I requested a non-smoking seat but on the plane found that I had been allocated a smoking seat. I pointed this out to the stewardess who immediately called the captain. On realising I was English he threatened to throw me off the plane and announced to the whole complement of crew and passengers that this is what you should expect from the English. It is about the only time I have travelled in a country with an openly hostile attitude to one's native land.

From there I went up to Paris to join Allan Leonard. I was to be his best man at his forthcoming wedding. We met at the auction of 2-year-olds held before the big spring races at Longchamps. On seeing Allan, I raised my beer glass just as a particularly valuable filly was up for auction. Fortunately, the auctioneer did not see my gesture or I might have found myself the proud but bankrupt owner.

Later that year Coca and I got married. The decision had been made to close the Chilean company and I was to visit MacLean, VA to discuss my future. I bought tickets that allowed us to stop at four different cities in the USA. We flew to Miami where we stored our winter bags and then to Paradise Island for the first leg of our honeymoon. We then went back to Miami to change bags and on to England to introduce Coca to my family and spend Christmas and New Year.

We returned once more to Miami, changed bags again and flew on to Jamaica for the third leg. This was less successful as we found the attitude of the hotel staff very unfriendly. It is my theory that socialism corrupts the service ethic. I had seen the changes in Spain before and after Franco's death. This is not to defend Franco but to simply observe that in a socialist country people are encouraged to think that the world owes them a living and this is particularly bad for the service industries.

So after one particularly rude waitress had spoilt another meal I asked my new bride whether she would like to go to New York. She immediately agreed and we checked out the following morning, returned to Miami to change back to winter bags and flew up to Kennedy. At Kennedy I phoned the New York Hilton who confirmed that they had a room and so we took a taxi there. Checking in, the desk clerk noticed that my British passport had been issued in Chile. He asked why and I told him, adding that I was on my honeymoon with my Chilean bride. He exclaimed, "But I am Chilean!" and insisted on upgrading us to the Bridal Suite. Needless to say, despite the New York winter we enjoyed that leg of our honeymoon very much.

Life with Coca gave me the opportunity to show her, Andrew and later Michelle much of what the UK had to offer. We developed a pattern of booking a country cottage in either the spring or autumn and taking a bucket-and-spade holiday further afield in the summer. We also liked to take the occasional city break and spend a weekend "doing" Florence or Paris. Over 37 years of marriage we have seen much of the world together, though there is always more to see.

Business travel depended on the company. With Crombie Eustace there were few opportunities, and not much more with Pillsbury, although it did give me a couple of chances to visit its Minneapolis/St Paul HQ and thus renew acquaintance with former Blake colleagues. I also had the chance to go to the Middle East for the first time. We had an excellent export business in Saudi Arabia and other Gulf countries and I visited these twice as part of our export efforts.

I found Saudi Arabia not much better than stepping back into the Middle Ages. Our distributor there, Abbar & Zainy, also owned a supermarket chain. The manager, Bob, was a British ex-pat who had been there too long. He had suffered a brain tumour and Sheik Abbar had flown him privately back to England for emergency surgery that had saved his life. Consequently Bob had a debt of gratitude that he felt could only be repaid by staying as long as Sheik Abbar wanted him. As the host employer also held the expatriate's passport, this was likely to be a long time. Bob showed me round Jeddah and from time to time would turn to me and ask me if I thought he was OK. There was a cartoon strip in circulation among the ex-pats that showed a Westerner turning progressively over 10 years into a monkey. Bob had been there seven. He told me of the time he had asked a boy to go and get some cigarettes for him.

"What brand do you want?" the boy had asked.

"Marlboro," replied Bob.

"What if they don't have Marlboro?" asked the boy.

"Oh! Get me anything."

So the boy came back with a cheeseburger.

I also went to Dubai, long before it became the tourist attraction it is now. Compared to Saudi it was civilised and welcoming to the Westerner. I needed to change my travel plans and went to a travel agent. Seated at the next stool was the owner of the agency. When he heard my name he revealed himself as also the owner of the company we had come to visit and promptly invited my export manager and me to his home for dinner. This was an unusual privilege. His home was not far short of a palace. The women were all hidden away and we were shown to a table made of rosewood at least 20 feet long and laden with food. There were just four of us. We spent the evening talking and eating with the right hand. (The left is for another bodily function.) I was full. Finally my host asked me if I would have some of the chicken. I reluctantly agreed. Then I asked him why he did not have some chicken.

"I don't like chicken!" was his reply.

At Sony there was much more opportunity to travel but it was a mixture of exciting business trips to Japan, boring business trips to Europe and marvellous incentive and conference trips to many thrilling locations around the world.

Most of the trips to Japan were for product-planning and were quite intense, with few opportunities for tourism. However, as these were often over two weeks I sometimes looked for adventure during the middle weekend. On one occasion I signed up for a one-day coach tour to Kamakura and Lake Hakone. from where you can see Mount Fuji. It took several hours to negotiate the horrible traffic jams to Kamakura, where there is a famous statue of Buddha. The guide gave us ten minutes to see the Buddha and we were off into the next jam to Hakone. We were due to have lunch there but were restricted to 15 minutes for lunch before getting on the boat across the lake. It was now getting dark and there was nothing to see. On the other side we went up to an art gallery which was closing and we had 5 minutes to see its treasures. Then it was back into the jam down the hill to the railway station. Then I took the train back to Tokyo. I got to my hotel at midnight having spent 16 hours travelling and less than half an hour sight-seeing.

That put me off similar excursions but on another occasion a group of us plucked up the courage to take the bullet train down to Hiroshima. We spent the night there and the following day visited the peace park. It is a memorable and imposing place and made a long-lasting impression.

I have countless photographs from my Sony years but often these were from snatched afternoons in the middle of a sales conference. More relaxing were those conferences where wives were included and Coca came with me to European conferences in Berlin, Venice, Seville, Biarritz, Gleneagles and finally Lisbon, where we made our farewells from the many friends we had made. She also joined me for UK conferences, and incentive trips in Cyprus, Bermuda, Florida, Penang, Thailand and a superb South Sea cruise around the Tahitian islands, thus allowing me to show her the beauties of Moorea and Bora Bora that I had visited on my own the year before we met.

Global roles with Pentland and NXT involved significant world travel but most of it was along familiar lines established with Sony. At Sony I had been able to sponsor dealer visits to Las Vegas, which I hated, while holding my own court for them in much more attractive places like Palm Springs, Santa Barbara and Maui. Later, one leading customer suggested that even the Las Vegas leg was no longer needed and we could hold our conferences wherever we wanted. Dixon's, my largest customer, got wind of this and its CEO, John Clare, pointed out his company rule that his staff could only visit company locations. "That's fine, John." I said. "Sony has factories all over the world!" and so we visited Penang, Bangkok and the Philippines in the next few years.

However, at NXT I was compelled to attend a number of exhibitions and conferences, several of which were held in Las Vegas. I went there eleven times in five years and swore that I really will never go back.

I have crossed the borders of some seventy-five countries but that still leaves about 125 more to see. There are many that I have no desire to visit even if the trip were paid for, but there are still so many that I would love to find time and money to see. A particular dream is to see all the UNESCO World Heritage Sites, nearly a thousand in all. However, they keep nominating new ones faster than I can get to see the existing ones so I will never fulfil that ambition.

DP in Hong Kong, 1998.

Six Degrees of Separation

"It's a small world, but I wouldn't want to have to paint it."
Stephen Wright (American actor and writer, b.1955)

"The Kevin Bacon Game".
At University my daughter, Michelle, played a game with her friends called the Kevin Bacon Game. The trivia game, Six Degrees of Kevin Bacon, is based on a variation of the concept of the small-world phenomenon and states that any actor can be linked, through their film roles, to actor Kevin Bacon. The game requires a group of players to try to connect any film actor in history to Kevin Bacon as quickly as possible and in as few links as possible. The game was played across various college campuses as early as the early 1990s.

Kevin Bacon is not a particularly distinguished actor but he's appeared in a lot of films with a lot of people and it is quite remarkable how few steps are needed to connect him with more established stars of a bygone era.

For example, Humphrey Bogart has a Bacon number of 2. Humphrey Bogart was in *The Wagons Roll at Night* (1941) with Eddie Albert. Eddie Albert was in *The Big Picture* (1989) with Kevin Bacon.

Cary Grant has a Bacon number of 2. Cary Grant was in *Charade* (1963) with Walter Matthau. Walter Matthau was in *JFK* (1991) with Kevin Bacon.

Charles Laughton has a Bacon number of 2. Charles Laughton was in *Forever and a Day* (1943) with June Lockhart. June Lockhart was in *The Big Picture* (1989) with Kevin Bacon.

Lucille Ball has a Bacon number of 2. Lucille Ball was in *Yours, Mine and Ours* (1968) with Stuart Nisbet. Stuart Nisbet was in *Murder in the First* (1995) with Kevin Bacon.

Rudolph Valentino has a Bacon number of 3. Rudolph Valentino was in *A Sainted Devil* (1924) with Jean Del Val. Del Val was in *Seven Thieves* (1960) with Eli Wallach. Eli Wallach was in *Mystic River* (2003) with Kevin Bacon.

Charles Chaplin has a Bacon number of 3. Charles Chaplin was in *A Countess from Hong Kong* (1967) with John Sterland. John Sterland was in *Dark Corners* (2006) with Michael J. Reynolds. Michael J. Reynolds was in *Where the Truth Lies* (2005) with Kevin Bacon.

Greta Garbo has a Bacon number of 3. Greta Garbo was in *Two-Faced Woman* (1941) with Ruth Gordon. Ruth Gordon was in *My Bodyguard* (1980) with Matt Dillon. Matt Dillon was in *Loverboy* (2005) with Kevin Bacon.

Originally put forward by American sociologist Stanley Milgram in 1967, the 'six degrees of separation' theory is that every person on earth can be linked to any other person by just six ties. He first argued that a person could maintain a social network of about 150 but through that network he could connect with the whole population of the USA, then *c.*150,000,000, in just six steps.

While Milgram's original experiment to prove his theory worked, it was conducted on a small scale. A random selection of just ninety-six people around the Americas had to reach their designated target through the US Mail. The messages that made it to their destination passed through an average of six people.

More recently, the Internet has allowed researchers to add significant weight to Milgram's theory. In 2003, a team at Columbia University asked 60,000 email users from 166 countries to reach one of eighteen target people in thirteen countries around the world. The average completed chain comprised just four people. However, having factored in the drop-out rate, the researchers calculated a median chain length of between five and seven people.

I play a variation on the Kevin Bacon Game, connecting myself to random figures in recent history. Thus I can connect to Stalin in 3, Mao Tse-Tung in 3, and Hitler in just 2. When I was a young salesman in

David Pearson

Sheffield I was driving in Derbyshire when the Duchess of Devonshire crashed her car into me. She had met Hitler as a young girl and of course her elder sister had been besotted with him. Churchill met Stalin at Yalta, Tehran and Potsdam and I have met several people who knew Churchill (2). Among the closest connections was Henrietta Spencer-Churchill who went out with Farad Azima, my first Chairman at NXT plc. Coca has a close relationship with Renato Poblete, a distinguished priest in Chile who runs a famous charity, Hogar Del Cristo. He has met Henry Kissinger (2) a number of times and Kissinger, of course, brokered rapprochement with Mao before setting up the famous meeting with President Nixon.

Among the Royals, I have never met the Queen, although I have seen her many times, first at my school on the occasion of its 450th anniversary, then countless times at Royal Ascot, and across a crowded lawn at her garden parties in Buckingham Palace. However, I have met all of her children a number of times. Of these I had the pleasure of working with HRH Prince Charles as a member of an advisory board to the Duchy of Cornwall, which led to the launch of Duchy Originals. Prince Charles, representing the Queen, will have met many of the world's leaders, including famously Robert Mugabe (2), as well as many other famous celebrities, including equally famously The Three Degrees. But then I have also met Sheila Ferguson. Royal connections can be a little obtuse. For example, I have met Princess Anne whose Aunt, Princess Margaret, knew Gore Vidal (3) who in turn knew Greta Garbo (4).

Eduardo Peña, a Spanish diplomat who befriended Carmen Bello and helped Coca when she lived in Spain, has met King Carlos, and that puts me just 3 from Franco. A Chilean friend of ours, Juanita Subercaseaux, the daughter of a diplomat, remembers sitting next to the son of Benito Mussolini (3) at school.

I met Pinochet when I lived in Chile, and Coca's mother knew Salvador Allende, who in turn knew Fidel Castro (3). Castro in turn had, of course, worked with Che Guevara (4). Tim Allan worked for Alistair Campbell at 10, Downing Street and then set up his own PR agency. He pitched for my business when I was at NXT and now includes President Putin (2) among his clients. Edward Heath came to meet me at Sony, and not long before had visited Iraq to try and mediate with Saddam Hussein (2) at the time of the first Gulf War.

Threads and Patches

Of the more legitimate generals, I can connect to Field Marshals Montgomery and Slim in just 2 and through them to most of the Second World War generals in 3. At school a young but already ambitious Michael Wood, who was to go on to find fame as a TV historian, engaged in correspondence in *The Times* defending Viscount Montgomery's version of events against the criticisms of Corelli Barnett. A delighted Monty (2) invited Mike down to have lunch at the House of Lords. Monty obviously worked with Eisenhower (3), Patton (3) and the rest. Many years later I also had lunch at the House of Lords and found myself sitting next to Viscount Slim, whose father, Bill Slim (2), had led the troops, including my father, in Burma. Slim later went to Australia as Governor General. His Prime Minister was the great Robert Menzies (3).

Continuing the political connections of recent Prime Ministers of Great Britain, I have met May, Blair, Major and Heath. Brown (2) has chaired a committee supported by my sister Angela and while I sadly never met Margaret Thatcher (2), I have met many who worked for her, including our former MP, Peter Lilley. Thatcher, of course, knew Reagan (3) and Gorbachev (3) among many others.

As a student in Minnesota I met Senator Charles Percy, who knew Nixon (2), and from there if you like we can go to John F. Kennedy (3) and Marilyn Monroe (4). My banker in Chile, Jim Callahan, met Jimmy Carter (2). More recently I met Martin Gilbert, Churchill's second official biographer, who took over from Randolph (2). Randolph was married to Pamela Harriman (3) who also married Averell Harriman (4).

Some more exotic connections can be made through Lord Howard of Rising, with whom I had lunch, who as a young man was Private Secretary to Enoch Powell (2). The wife of a long-term Chilean consul in London, Angelica Van Damm, had met Nelson Mandela (2).

Sir Leon Brittan came to Sony's HQ in Weybridge for tea one day. As European Commissioner he met Francois Mitterrand (2), who as a young politician had met General De Gaulle (3). Margaret Beckett also came to tea while in opposition. Later as Foreign Secretary (yes really!) she met Kofi Annan (2) and everyone else in the diplomatic world. Mrs Beckett also joined us for our 30th anniversary reception in Golden Square. Peter Mandelson and Peter Hain were also there. Peter Mandelson went on to become a European Commissioner, meeting up with Romano Prodi (2) and all the other European leaders, while Hain became Northern Island Secretary thus connecting us to the political leadership of the IRA, Gerry Adams and Martin McGuiness (2)

Meeting Foreign Secretary Rt Hon Margaret Beckett MP at Sony UK 30th Anniversary, June 1998.

Turning to the world of celebrities, it is easy to cut corners here while still playing within the rules of the game. If, for example, we have met one of the media interviewers who in turn has met everyone then the connections will be short. E.g. at Sony we sponsored the Radio Awards. Our compère for a number of years was Michael Aspel, who in turn has met a huge number of people on his chat show or as host of *This Is Your Life*. I have not met Michael Parkinson but I've met a few who have; e.g. Jimmy Tarbuck entertained a Sony Dealer conference once. Thus we can connect through those two to Fred Astaire (3), James Stewart (3) et al. At a Marketing Group of Great Britain dinner I met David Frost, who really did meet everyone. So here's just a few with whom I have a (2) via David Frost: Harold Wilson, James Callaghan, Margaret Thatcher, Gordon Brown, David Cameron, Gerald Ford, Ronald Reagan, George

H.W. Bush, Bill Clinton, George W. Bush, Oswald Mosley, Ian Smith, Mohammed Reza, Pahlavi, the last Shah of Iran, Benazir Bhutto, Daniel Ortega, Muammar Gaddafi, Vladimir Putin, A.J.P. Taylor, Rupert Murdoch, Sammy Davis, Jr., Tennessee Williams, John Cleese, Ronnie Barker and Ronnie Corbett.

Similarly, in sport, Desmond Lynam was a guest at the Sony Radio Awards once. He has interviewed many of the top sportsmen from Muhammad Ali (2) down. When I was playing football for New College, our college porter Tony Padley had a connection with Oxford United. They had done well, winning promotion from the old Southern League to the Second Division of the Football League in just a few seasons. Ron Atkinson was in that side, whom I later met in Thailand, but the manager was one Arthur Turner. Tony arranged for him to come along and coach us one evening. We were already in our kit but he just delivered a homily in a West Midlands monotone. "You start off with a draw" was one of his gems, and "You name them, I've played against them". I don't think he had heard of the Kevin Bacon Game but if he had I'm sure he could have helped me with Stanley Matthews, Tom Finney, Tommy Lawton and the rest. Anyway, it will all be in the record books somewhere. I have had a beer with Bobby Charlton, who played with Duncan Edwards (2); I have dined with Denis Law who played against Alfredo Di Stefano (2). Of that 1968 European Cup-winning side I have also met Brian Kidd and Alex Stepney, who famously saved from Eusebio (2), and I have enjoyed a drink with George Best, who Pelé (2) said was the best.

Pelé played against Geoff Hurst, whom I met at a sales conference; I worked with Alan Mullery, who played against Franz Beckenbauer (2); Emlyn Hughes who played against Johan Cruyff (2); and Terry Butcher who failed to stop Diego Maradona (2) from scoring.

In other sports I have met Nick Faldo, Ian Botham and Roger Black. Those three will connect me to any number of other famous sportsmen. I worked with Chris Brasher of Brasher Boot fame. I was on his Board for a while. Chris paced the first 4-minute mile for Roger Bannister (2). I knew Chris Bonington, the Everest climber, who climbed with most of the famous climbers of the last thirty years and outlived most of them.

In the Arts, I had a sherry with Ludovic Kennedy and stupidly said I had read his book. He politely asked, "Which one?" I think he has written around twenty. Ludovic is married to Moira Shearer (2), who must have danced with all the greats of her era and was directed in *The Red Shoes* by Michael Powell and Emeric Pressburger, who directed David Niven (4) in *A Matter of Life and Death*. (That's more like the Kevin Bacon Game.) Norio Ohga, my Chairman at Sony, had studied under Herbert Von Karajan (2) as a young baritone. He was at his deathbed. Von Karajan again connects us with leading Nazis but more interestingly with most of the top musicians of the last half of the 20th century, e.g. David Oistrakh (3), Sviatoslav Richter (3) and Mstislav Rostropovich (3), on one recording of the Beethoven Triple Concerto.

Meeting Sarah Ferguson, Duchess of York, at the Sony Radio Awards in 1989.
DP standing on left of Japanese Ambassador.

In jazz, I am indebted to Radio Awards for sitting me next to Humphrey Lyttelton, who knew Louis Armstrong (2). We were lucky enough to go backstage to meet Tony Bennett after a sensational concert at the Royal Albert Hall. Tony can connect us with Frank Sinatra (2), Ava Gardner (2) and the rest of that rat pack. Ned Sherrin was also a guest at Radio Awards and among many others, Ned knew Noël Coward (2). Another boy at my school, he was a few years senior to me but we shared a form room, was Robert Powell. At school he did a creditable *King Lear* (Mike Wood later did *Hamlet*!) and of course became famous as Jesus of Nazareth. However, he is less remembered for a bit part in *The Italian Job*. That connects me to Michael Caine (2) and, if you like, Lawrence Olivier (3) in *Sleuth*. Olivier was married to Vivien Leigh (4) who in turn starred with Clark Gable (5) in *Gone with the Wind*.

DP and Coca with Tony Bennett, Royal Albert Hall, 1997.

But I can get to Gable more cheaply. Michelle's University friend, Daisy, is related to Hedy Lamarr who played with Gable (3) in *Comrade X*. This kind of connection is more fun. How about Mrs Moes, the mother of Cristiaan who married Lucero, Coca's sister? We met her at the wedding in Holland. Mrs Moes had known Mrs Hepburn, the mother of Audrey (3).

Here's an example of how the game is played. Michelle's oldest friend, Johanna Beesley, set me the challenge of connecting to James Joyce. I was reading some books on holiday; one by John Simpson, the BBC reporter, mentioned a long-standing relationship he had had with Martha Gellhorn, one of Ernest Hemingway's wives. In the same book he mentioned Michael

Brunson, a rival ITV reporter whom I had met at a Sony event. Then on the same holiday I was reading a book by Ernest Hemingway in which he referred to meeting James Joyce in Paris. So there we have it DCP–Michael Brunson–John Simpson–Martha Gellhorn–Ernest Hemingway–James Joyce (5)

And I am holding the following up my sleeve. As a student at Oxford I worked one summer as an administrative assistant helping to organise an academic conference for NATO. This was attended by military and diplomatic representatives from all NATO countries and there were a few invited observers. The Israeli representative, Colonel Sion, was the daughter of Moshe Dayan (2), victor of the Six Days War. But I was particularly pleased to befriend a charming German diplomat, Freiherr Von Richthofen. His uncle had been the Red Baron himself, Baron Von Richthofen (2), the famous German First World War Air Ace, who would have had several medals pinned on his chest by Kaiser Wilhelm(3).

Part III

Diversions

Acting

> "All the world's a stage,
> And all the men and women merely players:
> They have their exits and their entrances;
> And one man in his time plays many parts."
>
> *As You Like It* – William Shakespeare

My mother was a fine amateur actress. She appeared in many local productions with the Townswomen's Guild, the Mothers' Union and later the Heald Green Theatre Club. When I was very young I had to be warned that she was making up to play the part of an old woman in Terence Rattigan's *Separate Tables* so that I would not be frightened. Her make-up must have been very good because years later, when she was old, she looked exactly like that, a beautiful young woman with old skin.

I was supposed to appear with her in Thornton Wilder's *Our Town*. There's a part for a young boy. He is on stage most of the time, but has no lines. Unfortunately this production was cancelled, so my debut was delayed. It was the 2nd Gatley Congregational Cubs who gave me my first starring role as a Native American chief. I nearly missed this, as it was that time of year when the clocks go back. Ours didn't so I turned up an hour early. I waited a long time and concluded that it had been cancelled; as that was the way with plays I appeared in. I went home, or rather to my grandmother's house as my parents were away. Some while later a man turned up in a car to collect me. How they traced me I do not know but I appeared as an out-of-breath Big Chief. The whole audience was on tenterhooks waiting for this first appearance in public.

Threads and Patches

Manchester Grammar School had a fine dramatic tradition and in my day I saw Robert Powell appear as King Lear with Russell Davies of Radio 4 fame as his Fool. Later, the TV historian Michael Wood practised his asides to camera in *Hamlet*. Intimidated by such company, I hung up my greasepaint. In my exchange year in the Blake School I attended some auditions for Shaw's *Androcles and the Lion* and found myself reading for the part of the Emperor. My British accent won the role and I thoroughly enjoyed myself, hamming it up with a scantily clad homecoming queen hanging on each arm.

The British accent was again featured as a butler to the wicked witches in *The Wizard of Oz*. This production was taken to the inner-city schools in Minneapolis, a marvellous experience. To see the poor black kids asking Dorothy about her flying was not to be missed.

At the end of the year we went on a bus trip through the United States. The bus stopped to stay in a number of communities from Keokuk, Iowa to Cattaraugus, New York. In each town we sang for our supper with a talent show. We were forty students from twenty-three nations and there was some talent, although it is remarkable how similar the national dances of the various cultures are. Of course the British contribute humour and with a French lad named Jean-Noel Fessy I got up a routine based on the simple question, "Have you seen the big green hat of the countess on top of the big green tree?" This was posed by Neanderthal man, by Italian opera singers, but what brought the house down was when Jean-Noel as President Charles De Gaulle put the question to the then Prime Minister, Harold Wilson.

In Midwest America my impression was obviously faultless, but it passed a sterner test when we came home by boat. The SS *Waterman* sailed from New York to Southampton and took nine days to complete the journey. We entertained ourselves with various games and shows and the sketch of the big green hat was revived. On the last day of the voyage we sighted the Scilly Isles and I remembered that that was where Wilson liked to holiday. I got on the ship's PA system and greeted the American Field Service students returning from their year in the USA. I said that if they looked over the port bow they would see me on the beach with my shrimp net. Sure enough, hundreds of international students rushed to wave to the British Prime Minister!

David Pearson

Pedigree Petfoods Sales Conference, 1979.

Of professional actors I have seen, the most celebrated was Sir Lawrence Olivier. I saw him play Ibsen's *The Masterbuilder*. It was somewhat spoilt by the deliberate pause for applause as he made his entrance, thus making the impression of someone giving a performance. Altogether more impressive was Dame Judi Dench, whom I have seen several times. She made a convincing Cleopatra opposite Sir Anthony Hopkins, a fine Countess of Rossillion in *All's Well That Ends Well* and a marvellous Ranyevskaya in *The Cherry Orchard*.

Hamlet is my favourite play. I studied it both at MGS and Blake, where I finished up teaching the teacher. I saw it performed by David Warner at the RSC, by Kenneth Branagh in his own Renaissance Company, by Simon Russell Beale at the National, and by Jude Law in the West End. In addition there were film versions by Olivier, the Russians and even Mel Gibson. Each sheds new light on a wonderful script. It is the exact opposite of the Japanese Kibuki theatre where the objective is to play it in exactly the same way for generations.

Also in Branagh's series was Dustin Hoffman as Shylock. Coca and I were in the front row and could see the great man spitting and yelling his way through Shakespeare's lines. As he apparently said at the time,

"You can't improvise this shit!" Other distinguished actors I have had the luck and privilege to see have included John Gielgud and Paul Eddington in *Forty Years On*, Jeremy Irons in *A Winter's Tale*, Jack Lemmon and Kevin Spacey in *Long Day's Journey into Night*, Derek Jacobi in *Breaking the Code*, *Beckett* (with Robert Lindsay) and *Richards II* and *III*, Alan Bates in *Melon*, Charles Dance as Coriolanus, John Wood as King Lear, Alan Alda in *Our Town*, Tim Pigott Smith in *Amadeus*, Kenneth Cranham in *An Inspector Calls* and *School for Scandal*, Denis Quilley in *The Merry Wives of Windsor*, Josie Lawrence in *The Taming of the Shrew*, Martin Shaw in *An Ideal Husband*, Edward Fox in *A Letter of Resignation* and *The Chiltern Hundreds*, Ray Fearon as Othello, Ian Hogg in *Julius Caesar*, Joseph Fiennes in *Love's Labour's Lost*, Tom Conti in *Jeffrey Bernard is Unwell*, Patrick Stewart in *The Tempest*, and with Sir Ian McKellen in *Waiting for Godot*, Henry Goodman and David Haig in *Yes, Prime Minister*, Kevin Spacey again in *Richard III*, Vanessa Redgrave and James Earl Jones in *Driving Miss Daisy*, Celia Imrie in *Noises Off*, Helen Mirren in *The Audience*, Anna Chancellor in *Private Lives*, Patricia Hodge in *Relative Values*, Antony Sher in *Henry IV Part II* and *King Lear*, Ralph Fiennes in *Man and Superman*, and David Threlfall in *Don Quixote*. If this looks like I have been chasing stars then I am sure I would have chased Bernhardt and Garrick in their day. Equally, I have seen many wonderful ensemble performances where the names of the actors don't resonate but their performances were on a par with all but the very best of those I have enumerated here.

Cowboys and Indians

"A four-legged friend, a four-legged friend,
He'll never let you down.
He's honest and faithful right up to the end,
That wonderful, one-two-three, four-legged friend."

Roy Rogers

As a boy my favourite game was Cowboys and Indians. In this respect I was like just about every other little boy growing up in the 1950s. At the beginning of the '50s few households had a television set. The Coronation in 1953 changed that and by the end of the decade most did, even if the majority were rented. The most popular TV programme genre was Westerns, both for children and adults. One of my earliest memories is watching TV in hospital while recuperating from a hernia operation. The programme was *The Cisco Kid*. There was also *The Lone Ranger*, *Bronco*, *Roy Rogers*, *The Virginian*, *Bonanza* and many more.

An early birthday present was a Davy Crockett outfit. This consisted of a Davy Crockett hat with an imitation racoon tail down the back and a jacket, together with a gun that fired caps. For a while even my mother called me Davy. Davy Crockett was a real-life American hero, a Tennessee backwoodsman who became a US congressman, and was then one of the martyrs who died at the Alamo. Thus he was not a cowboy but somehow this did not matter. In the legends of the Wild West the story of the United States expansion westwards was liberally interpreted. Rogues like Billy the Kid, Jesse James and Butch Cassidy were somehow seen as heroes just as Robin Hood is by the English. What was important was the simplicity of a fight between goodies and baddies. Goodies always wore light-coloured clothes with white hats. Baddies always wore black hats or were Indians in which case they were always bad, except Tonto, the Lone Ranger's sidekick, (so he wasn't alone).

The true history of the American colonisation of the Great Plains is undoubtedly one of great courage and fortitude. It also involves ethnic cleansing of epic proportions approaching genocide, as it does in much of colonial history.

But these moral issues were in the future for a little boy who needed heroes to aspire to in his play. Playing with toy guns was normal and great fun. What it did not do was give me any ambition to be a cowboy and ride a horse. My sister, Angela, went through the obligatory rite of passage of taking riding lessons but I did not seek to follow her example. Football took that place as we will see in another thread.

However, in 1968 I had the chance to be a cowboy, if just for a day. I was coming to the end of my year in America and a friend invited me to her father's ranch for the day. This ranch was a tax dodge, I understood, but a pleasant escape from the city. Four of us saddled up to take a bullock across the farm. The farm was large enough that the return journey took the best part of a day. My ride turned out to have a mind of his own. I had been on donkeys on the beach but had never ridden a horse before. I now found myself on a mustang who instinctively knew that I was not man enough to be his master, and no doubt had something of the Englishman about his riding style.

One canter turned into a gallop and I had no way of bringing this to a conclusion. We sped across fields and under trees. I wore no helmet and still think that the horse was trying to get me knocked off. But I hung on and after that he had a little more respect for me.

This was enough Cowboys, if no Indians, for a while, until in 1982 Coca and I got engaged in a mountain resort called La Leonera, some distance from Santiago. In our romantic mood we went riding the following day. I made a ring out of grass and we trotted gaily together through the foothills of the Andes on a beautiful spring day. Coca later told me she had been scared stiff but it was a delightful beginning to our engagement.

Then in 1995 we took a cottage in the hills of North Wales. I visited a Sony dealer in the town and he invited me to go riding with him. My daughter, Michelle, joined us and this time it was her turn to have the pony with a mind of his own. The tradition of Cowboys and Indians lives on.

Munich

"Oh! He's football-crazy, he's football-mad
And football's taken away the wee little bit of sense he had."

Robbie Hall and Jimmy MacGregor

In 1938 Neville Chamberlain flew to Munich for a shameful meeting with Adolf Hitler. His pathetic piece of paper really foretold of untold casualties in the inevitable war that followed. Munich became a synonym for appeasement. But for football fans everywhere Munich was to gain additional notoriety. Twenty years later, on 6th February 1958, Manchester United's chartered BEA Elizabethan failed to take off in the ice and snow and twenty-one people lost their lives, including eight players.

Although I was growing up in the Manchester area at the time, I was seven and I have no conscious memory of this tragic event. Incredibly, the surviving players and reserves fought through to reach a second successive FA Cup Final. I watched part of that but was more interested in forming a circus with friends in a neighbour's garden.

By the following year I had become a firm football fan and around that time decided I was a Manchester United supporter. I have changed my views on religion and politics since then, but that was never to change.

I was small for my age but fast, and although not particularly gifted, I taught myself dribbling and passing skills. This was at the expense of my father's roses and I grew expert in repairing plastic balls that had punctured on his thorns. I played my first representative games for the cubs and then the choir and finally the school. I played inside or outside left and was a regular for the second eleven at MGS.

Manchester Grammar School Under 14 2nd XI, 1963–64.
DP 2nd on left, front row.

My greatest success was in the USA. As an exchange student I was fortunate to be sent to a soccer-playing school. Blake had an average American football team but a pretty good record at soccer under a highly effective coach, Jack Fecht. The previous year the AFS student was a football wizard from Brazil. I had something to live up to.

Because of the severe winters in Minnesota the season was confined to the fall. We played a total of ten matches, just six of which were Conference.

We beat St Thomas Academy, Shattuck Academy (Marlon Brando's school) and Cretin. We drew with Breck and Benilde and came to the last game against Minnehaha with the classic situation where whichever school won would win the championship. By this time our matches were covered in the local press. Sport in American High Schools has a much higher profile than in the UK. I had scored eight of our twelve goals and my reputation had gone before me.

In the match I was closely marked: too closely as a red-headed chap kicked me every time I got the ball. Mr Fecht complained to the Russian referee at half-time but with little effect. Finally I scored, a not very elegant goal, bundling the ball in with my chest. The ref. disallowed it for handball and in frustration I kicked out at the redhead. I got him on both shins and he was substituted. Within minutes I had scored and then set up a second for our captain, Gregg Peterson. After the game I went up to the redhead, shook hands and congratulated him on his excellent play. We had won the Western Division Championship of the Minnesota High School League. I was awarded All-Conference Honours and voted Most Valuable Player by the coaches.

In celebration Jack Fecht said, "Why do people take drugs when they can get high like this?" and I knew what he meant.

At New College I was a regular in the first team, playing on the left of midfield in a 4-3-3 formation. We played in the first division and finished mid-table except in my final year when we were relegated. This upset me, as there was no opportunity for those of us who were leaving to get our place back. I tried out for the University team, probably the highest level I reached. I played as a lone striker against two strong centre halves. It was a good test of my work rate but little else. Years later I took a party to Rome to see England qualify for the World Cup. Dennis Tueart of Manchester City and England hosted our tour and over lunch we all lied about the highest level we had reached in our playing career, but I told the truth about this trial.

I first paid to watch a local team, Cheadle Rovers, and then a couple of representative schoolboy matches at Maine Road, which was just a bus ride from home. I even saw a Manchester City home game but I was a Manchester United fan and wanted to go to see them.

One Friday night in November 1961 I somehow upset my mother and was sent to my room to await punishment from my father. Instead I hid in a wardrobe with the ridiculous idea of suffocating myself. I was discovered and put in the dining room. I climbed out the window and ran away. I got as far as No. 20 (we lived at No. 4); my sister came after me and coaxed me back home. From thoughts of punishment my family realised that I must be an unhappy little boy and asked me what I would like to cheer me up. Instantly I replied that I wanted to go to Old Trafford to see Manchester United play.

The next day, Remembrance Day, my father took me and a friend to watch Manchester United draw 2-2 with Leicester City. Manchester United was then a shadow of the pre-Munich Busby Babes who nearly conquered Europe. The crowd was only 21,000 and it was an otherwise unmemorable match, but for me it was the start of something wonderful. From then on I seldom missed a home match. Entry to the groundside for Juniors was 1/6, a programme 4d and the train fare to Warwick Road 1/2. Thus, the whole day out was 3s (15p). Most of my pocket money went on this but as I gained confidence I also started to travel to some away games.

My father was marvellous and although he wasn't really a football fan, his own sport had been Rugby Union, he often drove me to important Cup games. The most important of these was the FA Cup Final of 1963. He bought two tickets the night before on the black market and drove us down on the morning of the match. Manchester United had had a poor season, only just avoiding relegation in the league. But their Cup form was totally different. I had seen all the matches except the 6th round and saw a great win over a fine Leicester City side with the unparalleled Gordon Banks in goal. David Herd scored two and the new star, Denis Law, the third.

The next season I saw George Best make his debut and from then on the fabulous trio of Best, Law and Charlton inspired a truly great team to win the league in 1965 and 1967. In 1965 I ran on the pitch to celebrate, the first time I had been on the sacred Old Trafford turf.

Ironically I was away in America in 1968 when Matt Busby finally achieved his ambition – to be the first English team to win the European Cup. Ten years after the first team had died in the attempt, a team that incredibly featured two survivors from Munich, Bobby Charlton and Billy Foulkes, had won the Cup.

After reaching that pinnacle the team went into decline and the extraordinary gifts of George Best were thrown away. Little success was won but I never lost my enthusiasm and even saw several of the matches they played in the old second division in 1974–75.

In the 1990s the glory years returned, driven by the strength of another Scot, Alex Ferguson, with the charismatic Eric Cantona on the pitch. Rumbelows sponsored the League Cup and their Buying Director, Bill Cosgrove, a keen Manchester United fan, asked Sony to sponsor a Man of the Match award. I agreed and Bill invited me to see some great performances against Liverpool (3-1), Arsenal (6-2) and Leeds (3-1 on aggregate). At one of these I presented the Man of the Match award to Mark Hughes. This was the second and last time I appeared on the

Old Trafford pitch. After the match we were invited to the Boardroom where Sir Bobby Charlton offered me a cup of tea and Denis Law a whisky. In the final we sat in the Royal Box with the politicians and other dignitaries. The most impressive of these for me was a very old Sir Matt Busby.

I met more of my childhood heroes when Sony came up with a new way of entertaining our top dealers. We flew them to a resort in Thailand and secretly flew out top football stars: Peter Bonetti, Terry Butcher, Emlyn Hughes, Denis Law, Rodney Marsh, Alan Mullery, Terry Neil, Martin Peters and manager Ron Atkinson. Playing in teams, we competed in football knowledge. This formula was repeated back in England with other groups of dealers and at one of these I got to meet George Best. He was by now a sad drunk but still a great hero. I told him I had seen his first game but, of course, he had heard that from so many people that there must have been half a million in the stadium.

The night before a match in London, Alex Ferguson usually stayed with the team, but on one occasion, in January 1997, he and I had dinner together with Bobby Campbell, who had managed George Best at Fulham, and Max Morgan, one of Sony's marketing consultants. This was just when Kevin Keegan had resigned suddenly from the managership of Newcastle United. Because we had tried to book him for our event in Thailand I knew what the press didn't, that Kevin was in hiding, playing golf in Florida, and I told this to Alex. He put this in a diary of the season he published, but I must have made a mixed impression on him as he referred to me as David Gibson, head of Sony, Europe. The following season he invited me to one of the games at Old Trafford. I took Coca, Andrew and Michelle, and afterwards we went to his inner sanctum for a drink with his more intimate friends.

After I left Sony I joined Pentland and the sporting links remained strong. One customer, Allsports, was a sponsor of Manchester United and they invited me to fly with the team to a European game in, of all places, Munich. Unfortunately, I could not travel with the team but travelled out on the day of the match. The team was due to fly back straight after the match and so I travelled without baggage. We were superbly entertained, including by Sir Bobby Charlton, and then came the match against Bayern Munich. I had been outside the Olympic Stadium after the terrorists had ruined the 1972 Games. United played well, could have won, and finally came away with a 2-2 draw. Then we found that there was a problem with the plane. The authorities would not let it land. We were forced to stay in the city of Munich after all. The following morning we all flew back to Manchester together, safely.

At the end of the season these same two teams battled through to the final. I arranged for our son, Andrew, who was working for the Speedo distributor in Barcelona, to get a ticket. I was forced to watch it with some Pentland people on a 14" TV in a hotel in Halifax. The last two minutes of that match must be the greatest in sport. United, without their suspended inspirational captain, Roy Keane, had been pedestrian. Ferguson, in that enigmatic way, had picked a strange team. But inspired substitutions came off and first Sheringham and then Solskjaer put the ball in the Germans' net. They returned to Munich empty handed.

DP with son Andrew and Alex Ferguson, Old Trafford, May 1998.

DP with Brian Robson, Captain of Manchester United and England, after Rumbelows Cup 3rd Round – Manchester United 3 - Liverpool 1. October 1990. Sony sponsored the Man of the Match.

Singing

"Pussy said to the Owl, 'You elegant fowl!
How charmingly sweet you sing!
O Let us be married! Too long we have tarried:
But what we shall we do for a ring?'"

                      "The Owl and the Pussy-Cat" – Edward Lear

St Catherine's Church Choir. DP first on left in front row, *c*.1964.

As a boy I had a good treble voice, and sang in several choirs. There was the choir of St Catherine's Church, for which I auditioned at about nine and stayed for five years as my voice refused to break. Indeed it never did in the spectacular way that happened to some boys I knew. Rather it just slipped gradually downwards until it became a pleasant baritone. I also sang in the school choir at Manchester Grammar School and in the more select Memorial Hall Choir. This would have the honour of singing in the cathedral choir benches on Founder's Day. I also sang in Chester Cathedral as one of a select few sent for further training.

My first paid employment was as a choirboy. We were paid quarterly depending on attendance, and would receive about 15 shillings. However, weddings paid much better and we would each receive half a crown for a wedding. We paid special attention to the reading of the banns in church, hoping that these fine couples would be persuaded by the vicar to have a full choir for their ceremony. Funerals reputedly paid 3/6 but I never knew of this experience. This was probably just as well as boys of this age are not known for their solemnity.

I sang my share of solos and the best of these was the first verse of the carol "Once In Royal David's City". This had been popularised in The Festival of Nine Lessons and Carols that was broadcast every Christmas Eve from King's College, Cambridge. Not to be outdone, we had our own version of this and the church would be packed for this service, a week or so before Christmas. The solo is the first act of the service and traditionally is sung as a processional from the back of the church. I was intensely nervous and found it hard going in the early part of the verse. Then on the glorious notes of the last two lines my confidence returned and I soared up to the top notes with great satisfaction.

At Blake School I joined its Glee Club, a well-run group of boys' voices. By now I was baritone and again I was given the solo for a rendition of "I'll go no more a rovin'." We toured in the Midwest, performing concerts in Iowa, Oklahoma and Kansas City. We performed here at a girls' school and there was a mixer afterwards. That night Martin Luther King was assassinated less than 400 miles away in Tennessee. The black communities in many major cities in the South rioted and our bus was shot at. We spent the journey lying on the floor and were warned not to go on the balconies of our motel rooms.

At Oxford I became a great friend with David Hughes, an Englishman whose parents had moved to Kirkcaldy in Fife. Dave had picked up many of the Scottish folk songs, I knew many of the English and we decided to see how many songs we knew. We stayed up all night going through our repertoire of folk and pop. Our rules were that we had to think of a new song within one minute or give up. We were still going at breakfast and had reached a total of 600. Hysteria set in when, almost stuck, I came up with a rendition of "Champion, the Wonder Horse".

My finest hour as a singer came in Chile. I used to visit a pub called New Orleans. It was expensive but served good food and drink. Most Saturday nights a local amateur jazz band entertained with some very creditable traditional jazz. One night I was surprised to see a member of the audience get up to sing a couple of numbers. The following week I talked with some of the band and they asked me to join them.

DP singing jazz in New Orleans pub in Santiago, Chile, August 1982.

I sang "When the Saints Go Marching In" in my best imitation of Satchmo. Soon after, I was introduced to the girl who would become my wife. Her sister, Lucero, who introduced us, told Coca to bring her camera and so I have a photographic record, though sadly no musical record, of this gig.

Though musical I never learnt to play an instrument, one of my genuinely few regrets. As a small boy my father suggested I should learn to play the piano. I did not feel that I wanted to do so and declined. Some years later, a little more mature, I told him I was now ready to learn the piano. He snapped, "You had your chance." My younger brother, Andrew, made no such mistake and learnt to play very well. He had a particular talent for playing Scott Joplin's rag which had been popularised as the music from *The Sting*.

I nevertheless loved music and became a keen pop music fan. As a teenager I went to a few local dances with ordinary groups who could strum their three chords and cover Chuck Berry and other Rock'n'Roll standards. Then in the USA, as with so many other things, I started to spread my wings and saw a few proper concerts including Peter, Paul and Mary, Glen Campbell and Sergio Mendes' Brasil '66. At Oxford I continued this and went to reasonably low-cost clubs where blues groups like Free were building their University fan base. With a group of friends, and with Ian Black as driver, I went to rock festivals at Hollywood (a field in Staffordshire) and Bath (another field in Somerset). These were the forerunners of much bigger festivals at Glastonbury and the Isle of Wight but gave me the chance to see Led Zeppelin, Carlos Santana and many other big names of the day. Another concert I attended was the inaugural concert of Blind Faith, a super group put together by Eric Clapton of Cream and Stevie Winwood of Traffic. This was held in Hyde Park and I hitch-hiked to London with Paul Wait to see it. Well, we heard it but did not see it as the concert was so over-attended that the park was full and we could get nowhere near the stage.

My sister, Angela, had more luck when attending a May ball in Oxford. Featured at her ball was the great John Mayall with his Bluesbreakers, which had launched so many careers of British Blues stars including Peter Green, Mick Fleetwood and John McVie of Fleetwood Mac, Mick Taylor of the Rolling Stones and Andy Frazer of Free. And, of course, the legendary Eric Clapton. Eric was playing at a rival ball that night with Cream but wandered round to hear his mentor play. On seeing him Mayall cried out "Eric! Have you got your gui-tar?"

Eric said no he'd left it but Mayall was not to be denied. "Give the man a gui-tar," and the audience was treated to an impromptu set from the two greatest blues musicians this country has produced.

During the 1970s I would see the occasional concert with the Hollies, Elton John, Slade and other contemporary groups. The best of these was a concert by Frankie Valli and the Four Seasons. Frankie Valli has an amazing vocal range covering four octaves but he also has fabulous charisma. When he completed his last number the audience of course yelled for more. He handled them with great skill saying:

"You want more?"

"More!" came back the cry.
"You want more?"
"MORE!"
"We weren't going anyway," and they proceeded to sing four more songs with great panache.

But I gave up this kind of activity when at Sony we had sponsors' tickets to see Michael Jackson at Wembley. It was Michelle's first concert and she suffered from the terrible noise, as we all did. Jackson kept everyone waiting for over an hour while they played Beatles songs, to which, of course, he owned the rights. His concert was awful with a terrible sound system that echoed inside the stadium and several times drove me out in to the corridors for relief from actual physical pain.

No doubt this is partly age-related but I actually believe video did kill the radio star. When video came in in the late 1970s, pop music was promoted by video on MTV and the like rather than on the radio. Thus the emphasis was on selling an image rather than a sound and often the sound was of staggeringly low quality.

I loved jazz and all its derivatives except perhaps the more atonal jazz of the late 1950s. There were some most enjoyable evenings in The Bull at Barnes with my mother's cousin, John Wyatt, featuring Humphrey Lyttelton, Kathy Stobart and other stalwarts of British jazz.

George Melly was a great entertainer whom I saw a number of times with John Chilton's Feetwarmers. In the US I saw the great George Shearing and, back in the UK with Coca, saw Buddy Rich support Frank Sinatra. We saw Sinatra twice, the second time with Liza Minnelli and Sammy Davis Jr, all terrific entertainers. Sinatra is on his own and though we saw him towards the end of his career he was still the supreme interpreter of a song, to the extent that usually once Sinatra sang a song it was finished for everyone else. There were exceptions and it was also a great thrill to see Tony Bennett when he was still at the top of his powers. He at one point used the full acoustics of the Albert Hall by asking for the amplification to be switched off and singing beautifully a capella, filling the hall without difficulty. Coca and I were invited to meet him afterwards and found him both modest and charming.

Stage musicals are some of the best entertainment around. When a good writer meets a fine composer the results can be fabulous. I have seen most of the famous musicals and my particular favourite has been a chance to see an ageing but still mesmerising Rex Harrison as Professor Higgins in *My Fair Lady*. The actress playing his mother was only a few years older than him.

Coca and I saw early performances of *Phantom of the Opera*, *Les Misérables* and *Miss Saigon* with most of their original casts intact. In contrast we adored a revival of *Forty Second Street* with a 16-year-old Catherine Zeta Jones as Peggy Sawyer.

I had always loved classical music just as much. There were a few records in the house where I grew up and we went to some concerts. At a very young age I was taken to hear David Oistrakh play at Belle Vue, and then in my teens I witnessed Jacqueline Du Pré's legendary performance of Elgar's Cello Concerto, conducted by her husband, Daniel Barenboim with the Hallé Orchestra in the Manchester Free Trade Hall. In the US, my American "mother", Mary Hannah, was associated with the excellent Minneapolis Symphony Orchestra and I particularly remember an impressive virtuoso display by Christian Ferras.

Opera would come, I knew. I was familiar already with some of the music and started to build up a small collection of some of the highlights from Verdi, Puccini and Wagner. Then, at Sony, Coca and I were invited to the Royal Opera House for the first time. The opera, Cherubini's *Médée*, was not the most distinguished in the canon, but the occasion, the sense of theatre, the appeal to so many of the senses, all overwhelmed me and I decided to take this up in earnest. I persuaded Sony to become Full Members of the ROH, thus guaranteeing access to good tickets, and over the next ten years this became my principal form of customer entertainment. Coca and I saw nearly a hundred performances of around ninety operas and ballets. We saw just about all the popular operas with most of the leading performers of the day, including all of the Three Tenors and several of their leading prima donnas.

We have a particular love for Puccini and have seen Tosca no less than eight times, including both Domingo and Pavarotti as Cavaradossi. By now Pavarotti was so huge that in the first act he was too heavy to climb the artist's ladder and paint the eyes of Tosca. In the third act, when he is executed, he fell down in instalments before expiring. But he could still sing like an angel.

Pavarotti was the better singer – indeed, probably the best of his generation – but Domingo was the better actor. We saw him also play opposite Mirella Freni in *Fedora*, with Kiri Te Kanawa in *Otello*, and brilliantly as Cyrano de Bergerac.

However, our most memorable night with Domingo was not in the Opera House but in the royal palace at Seville. At a Sony European Management Conference we were shown into a courtyard where a piano waited on a stage. Eventually a representative of Sony Music explained that Placido Domingo, who was Artistic Director of the Seville Expo at the time, would sing for us.

He came onto the stage with his accompanist and started to sing. Immediately all the birds also burst into song. Domingo said that he would be singing duets tonight and proceeded to sing his favourite zarzuelas. Afterwards Coca made sure of being photographed with him and he made great compliments about the beautiful women of Chile.

Cricket

"Cricket, lovely cricket."

West Indian calypso

Cricket may be the greatest game in the world. Football is the world's game and the beautiful game. It arouses more passion and I would certainly get more excited about Manchester United or England winning their respective international competitions. But for its variety, its grace, its athleticism, for the way in which it more closely reflects life, cricket wins every time.

It is a very difficult and technical game. Its rules are not simple; there are many stories about the difficulty of explaining the game to a foreigner, particularly an American. However, in many parts of the world, particularly the former colonies of the British Empire, it is the number-one sport, even the number-one subject of interest. An international match between India and Pakistan will attract a greater TV audience than the so-called World Series in Baseball.

The English had a talent for codifying the sports and pastimes that they played in their public schools. Thus football, rugby, tennis, boxing, athletics, golf and many others were exported around the world through the military and then the trading empires of the British. Some sports were picked up abroad and re-exported, such as polo and badminton. But cricket has a unique history.

Competitive cricket was being played in the 18th century, and by the middle of the 19th it was professional. Though in that unique British manner, for more than another century many of the participants declined to be paid and described themselves as "Gentlemen" to distinguish themselves from the professional "Players".

The first international match was played between England and Australia in 1877 on Melbourne Cricket Ground. Australia won – not much change there then. [This was written before the historic Ashes series of 2005.] International cricket is now played all over the world between several countries and can arouse great feelings. The 1932–33 series in Australia against England, known as the "Bodyline" tour because the England captain asked his bowlers to bowl at the bodies of the Australian batsmen in a tactic to defeat the incomparable Don Bradman, caused diplomatic incidents in a way that even the "Hand of God" by Diego Maradona could not replicate in the 1986 World Cup. In the 1960s and '70s, cricket became the principal tool by which pressure was brought to bear on the Apartheid regime in South Africa. In the West Indies, cricket is the one way in which otherwise disparate islands can express their unity. In Zimbabwe, it was unfortunately used by the despicable Robert Mugabe to show that his country could have normal relations with the rest of the world.

As I grew up I tried to teach myself the game. I read avidly the biographies of the great players such as Don Bradman and Peter May and they claimed to have taught themselves. My father bought me a complete set of wickets and bails as well as bat and ball. Day after day I set these up in our garden but our lawn was only 11 yards long and a full cricket pitch is twice that. In teaching myself to bowl the perfect length in our garden it was impossible to adapt to a normal pitch. Well, that's my excuse anyway.

At school, in loosening up for a form match, I took a cricket ball full in the mouth. My lips blew up like a balloon but the following day I climbed Snowdon with my father and some friends. At a school camp in Manorbier near Tenby in South Wales we played mallet cricket. I hit the ball over a fence and in retrieving it caught my leg on the barbed wire. I was rushed to hospital on the back of a motorbike and had stitches without any anaesthetic. I still bear the scar.

Other than these pathetic experiences I have very few memories of playing cricket at school, but at New College, Allan Leonard organised an unofficial college team he called the Incogniti. We enjoyed a variety of matches against a mixture of opposition. Our own standards varied according to the quality of our opposition. Allan would put me on to bowl when he wanted the other side to score some runs. On one occasion I ran in from the boundary in feeble imitation of a fast bowler. I hurled the ball in the direction of the stumps and to my amazement shattered them. Allan came up to me and said, "What on earth are you doing? I don't want to get them out yet." I made up for it with a series of overthrows from the field.

My only other cricket over twenty years has been two matches. At Green's, the management played the staff in a game on the pitch next to our Thurcroft factory. I was bowled first ball for a duck but took three wickets and a catch and elected myself Man of the Match. Our accountant took excellent photos from the boundary and I sent one of my dismissals to the Primary Club. This is a charity that raises funds for blind cricketers. To qualify for membership you have to have been out first ball in any kind of cricket.

DP joining the Primary Club, bowled first ball in match at Thurcroft, 1987.

The other was for the charity Birthright (now Wellbeing) in a match against the Gynaecologists and Obstetricians at Victor Blank's magnificent private ground. By this time I was finding a simple game of cricket a test of muscles I never knew I had.

The first professional cricket I saw was the 1960 test match against South Africa at Old Trafford. Soon after, I joined Lancashire as a student member and for 12/6 (that is twelve shillings and sixpence in old money or 62.5p) had a season ticket for all matches in the season. On several Saturdays I went to Old Trafford to see Lancashire play. However, born in Surrey, I considered myself a Surrey supporter, no doubt influenced by the fact that they had won the County Championship for the previous six seasons with great players like Peter May, Alec Bedser and Jim Laker. On holiday on the south coast I persuaded my father to take me to see Hampshire play Surrey at Southampton and saw this magnificent team before it broke up.

Over the years I have seen test cricket at all the main venues: Old Trafford, Edgbaston, Trent Bridge, Lord's and The Oval, except Headingley in Leeds. The nearest I got to Leeds was in 1975 when I stayed in the same hotel as the Australians. The great Dennis Lillee and Jeff Thomson were trying to hit golf shots over the hotel. The media were also staying there and the legendary commentator John Arlott had dinner with his Australian counterpart Alan McGillivray at the next table. True to his reputation as a vinophile he ordered the wines (three of them) before even looking at the food menu. The match was abandoned as a draw after vandals campaigning for the release from prison of a convicted criminal sabotaged the pitch with knives and oil.

More recently I contented myself with an annual visit to Lord's to see the Saturday of the Lord's test. That way I kept in touch with the game and saw most of the top players. On one occasion I tried to interest Coca in the game. We had tickets for a great occasion. To celebrate the bicentenary of the MCC in 1987, an MCC side played a Rest of the World side with some of the greatest players of the day on show. Unfortunately, it rained heavily overnight and although the rain had stopped we had to wait for the outfield to dry before the umpires would permit play to start. Eventually we saw a couple of hours' play in the afternoon but only after watching grass dry for several hours. This put Coca off cricket for life.

The Marketing Society used to run a scheme called Market Aid where members would offer their services to charities pro bono. I had previously helped the CEO of Children Nationwide, a medical charity, think though her strategy and was asked to perform a similar role for Tom Rodwell, the Chairman and Chief Executive of the London Community Cricket Association (LCCA). This had been formed as one of the many knee-jerk political responses to the Brixton riots in the 1980s. However, unlike most of the others, this one had stuck. Black kids from rough neighbourhoods were coached in the game of cricket. For many it worked, perhaps because it is a non-contact sport, perhaps because you don't have to be of a particular physical type to play. Indeed, while top fast bowlers are usually big powerful men, many of the world's top batsmen are small with a low centre of gravity and the ability to quickly move into position and play the ball as late as possible; think of Sashin Tendulkar and Brian Lara, the two greatest batsmen of the modern era. Perhaps it works because so many of the role models are also black. The Caribbean has produced many of the finest cricketers and the sport is the national game throughout India, Pakistan and the rest of the subcontinent.

LCCA developed three strands – it continues to teach the game to poor kids from underprivileged backgrounds and some of these have come through to play county cricket. In addition it teaches blind and disabled cricket. With this background it has found an international role, sponsored by the Foreign and Commonwealth Office in bridging diplomatic gaps in places from Afghanistan to Zimbabwe where normal channels have failed. It even played a role in Cuba where sport is playing a proxy for the fight for influence after the Castros. The US will use baseball and the British and the Commonwealth, cricket.

I spent a happy summer with Tom watching both 20/20 games at Lord's and competitive youth games at other top grounds while we thrashed out the priorities of this unusual and worthwhile charity, which we renamed Cricket for Change. Tom later published a wonderfully positive book about his experiences with this charity. He called it *Third Man in Havana* and even got Graham Greene's widow's permission to use the title. (This story is covered in more detail in one of my blogs in the section on Foreign Affairs later in the book.)

In 2006, a new ambassador from Chile, H.E. Rafael Moreno, came to London. At a Christmas party of the Anglo-Chilean Society he asked me to explain the laws of cricket. I did my best but followed this up by inviting him to a test match as the best way of learning. He came with me to watch England play South Africa at the home of cricket, Lord's, in 2008, a match which England dominated, but South Africa, following on, made nearly 400 for the loss of just 3 wickets to save the game. Rafael lived up to the occasion by introducing Chilean wine to all our neighbours in the stand.

Messing About in Boats

"Believe me, my young friend, there is nothing – absolutely nothing – half so much worth doing as simply messing about in boats."
The Wind in the Willows – Kenneth Grahame

No part of the British Isles is more than 75 miles from the sea. A desire to visit it, look at it, paddle in it, swim in it and finally cross it is deep rooted in British consciousness. For those of us who grew up in the 1950s a bucket-and-spade holiday was an essential feature in the calendar.

As well as the bucket and spade, a toy boat was also de rigueur. We used to have a model yacht based on the Endeavour series. At weekends we would go to Lindow Common where there was a small lake and sail it across the lake. Then in the summer of 1959 we took a holiday at Criccieth in North Wales. My mother was expecting my brother, Andrew, and my father only joined us for the weekend. We were sailing the yacht in the shallows when the wind took it out to sea. My father, a very strong swimmer, swam out after it but though he swam several hundred yards he had to give it up and came back safely, to the intense relief of all of us. I often wondered how far round the world that little toy yacht travelled.

My first experience sailing in a real boat was with the Senior Scouts. On one trip we stayed on Combs Reservoir in Staffordshire and were taught how to row properly. I even received a certificate for this feat. I have never forgotten the command "Toss oars!" on which you pull in your oar, hoist it up in the air and then bring it down flat in the boat all in one movement. On another we stayed on Lake Windermere, the largest inland water in England, and did some basic sailing. More memorable was when Neil Culliford and I rowed across the lake and discovered a large metal container. It floated, and with a makeshift oar, Neil steered it back across while I brought in the real boat.

Combs Reservoir.

Neil Culliford on Lake Windermere.

David Pearson

In 1967 I went to live with the Hannahs in Minnesota as an exchange student. They had a lovely house on Lake Minnetonka. Minnesota is known as the Land of Ten Thousand Lakes. There are actually closer to 40,000 but Minnetonka is one of the largest, with miles of shoreline and innumerable bays. We had a motorboat, which during the summer months was a great source of fun, though, as with snow skiing, I found that water skiing and I did not go together.

Despite my certificate in rowing, I was not attracted to the sport at Oxford. Perhaps unfairly, I associated it with the Hooray Henry crowd. College sports were financed by a levy on all students. The budget was then fought over by the different sports captains. The college boats were easily the most expensive sporting assets and replacement would absorb most of the total annual budget. It became a great focus of contention, particularly as so few participated in the sport compared with the more popular games of football, rugby and cricket.

However, I do have many happy memories of punting in my student days. Punting is the essence of messing about in boats. There should be no competitive aspect to it, although there were occasions when we raced back from up-river pubs.

Peter Morris was a good friend at New College and his father had converted half a pontoon raft into a serviceable canal-going vessel. With another friend the three of us enjoyed a four-day trip from Wolverhampton down to Stourport and back on the Staffs and Worcester Canal. The whole time we were within five minutes' walk of a bus ride back to Wolverhampton. But it was a different world, relaxing and peaceful. Even when we passed through a major town we saw it from a different perspective.

Some years later, on the same river as I had learnt my punting, John Eustace, who had recently joined Pedigree Petfoods from Procter & Gamble at the same time as me to be my line manager in the Thames Region, planned an away day for the management team in a hired cruiser. He and I drove from Goring, where John lived, to Oxford to pick up the boat and a barrel of beer. We then planned to take the boat back down to Goring to meet the rest of the team that evening. A journey of 13 miles by road had taken 30 minutes. However, the same journey by river was a) much more than 13 miles and b) would take much more than 30 minutes. It took all day and we needed to exceed the speed limit of 4 miles per hour. Fuelled by the beer, we arrived in Goring late in the evening, having negotiated the last few locks without official assistance.

With Sony, Pentland and NXT there have been enjoyable days sailing in the Solent. I organised another away day for my management team at Sony and we set up a race between two Sunsail yachts. Such was the competitiveness of the Sony management that both crews claimed victory. At Pentland a colleague, Nick Webster, invited Coca, Michelle and me to join him and his wife for a delightful summer day's sailing across to the Isle of Wight and back. Then I again organised an away day for the NXT management team, hiring Jon Vizor's boat, a beautiful craft that had been designed by Farad Azima.

Sailing Jon Vizor's yacht with the NXT team on the Solent, 2000.

Over the years these occasional forays into boating, combined with similar excursions when on holiday in places like Cyprus, Mauritius, Sardinia and Tahiti and others, have kept a dream alive that one day I will have my own boat. The emotional side of me expresses this desire quite strongly. The rational side of me says that it will be like standing in the shower and tearing up fifty-pound notes.

Nevertheless, it was with great pleasure that we bought our apartment in Chile overlooking the Club de Yates de Higuerillas, a very exclusive yacht club in a marvellous location by the Pacific.

Club De Yates, Higuerillas, Chile. View from our apartment.

We later sold the apartment because of cost. It would have cost thousands of dollars to join the yacht club and we would probably have only used it once or twice a year.

And there is cruising. We took our first cruise back in 1995 when I worked for Sony and every year we would set our independent dealers sales targets. If they achieved these they could go on holiday with the company, led by a group of Sony personnel. I was fortunate enough to go to some extremely nice places but perhaps the highlight was a cruise on the *Windstar* round the Society Islands, starting off in Tahiti and calling in at Huahine, Raiatea, Bora Bora, Moorea and then returning to Papeete to take it easy before flying back to London via Los Angeles. This was a marvellous start to our cruising life, or perhaps spoilt us, as under our own steam I doubt whether we would have been able to afford this.

We took it up again in 2011, this time with Fred Olsen. This cruise was to the Baltic Sea from Southampton. We sailed in the *Balmoral* up the North Sea, through the Kiel Canal and called in at Tallinn in Estonia, St Petersburg in Russia and Helsinki in Finland, culminating in Copenhagen in Denmark and Kristiansand in Norway. One of the marvellous things about such tours is that you only pack and unpack and repack once, even though you're calling in at so many places. The food and wine and entertainment were also most enjoyable and we made good friends if not lifetime friendships with the people with whom we shared a table.

Our next cruise was round much of the eastern Mediterranean and this was less successful. The places we visited were good, starting from Rome and its port Civitavecchia, then Messina in Sicily from where we went towards Mount Etna; Piraeus in Greece from where we saw Athens; Kusadasi from where we saw Ephesus in Turkey: Chania in Crete and then back to Civitavecchia to fly back from Rome. Unfortunately, this time we had chosen a large American ship and we found their highly commercial attitude much less sympathetic than the British style of Fred Olsen. They were always trying to sell something; they made us go through the casino to get anywhere; they would always greet you for breakfast in a loud and almost aggressive way; and, of course, it was a multinational passenger base and while one should not complain about that it meant that every announcement was in several languages, even starting quite early in the morning when you were getting up in your cabin. So never again for us with that kind of cruise ship.

The following year we went on our first river cruise, this time on the Rhine. So we took a train to Paris and then to Basel where we picked up our ship. We travelled north through Switzerland, visiting Lucerne and Interlaken; then into Germany, driving by coach through the Black Forest and across into France to see Strasbourg; cruising back into Germany to see Speyer and Rudesheim; then through the famous Rhine Gorge. We then called at Koblenz, and our last stop, Cologne, then returning through the Netherlands to Brussels and back to London on the Eurostar. A river cruise has the same advantage as a sea cruise in that you see many different places but only pack and unpack once. But it has the added advantages that your view is constantly changing as you travel through the day, and also it is a much smaller ship with perhaps 150 passengers, so everything is smaller in scale and more intimate.

We took another sea cruise up the North Sea with Fred Olsen, this time just concentrating on the fjords of Norway. We visited several of the most beautiful fjords in the world. We were back in a medium-size ship with good food and entertainment and some fine excursions when we stopped. The next year we took another river cruise, this time in France, concentrating on the Rhone. We took the train all the way down to Avignon, then joined the boat to see Arles, Vienne, Beaune, and finally Lyon. In all we picked up five World Heritage sites on this cruise including some of the finest in the world, like the Pont du Gard, probably the Romans' greatest architectural achievement.

The following year we took yet another river cruise, this time on the Douro in Portugal. We started in Porto, where we took the boat west through Pinhao, then Vega de Terron, from where we took a coach trip to Salamanca in Spain and back to Pocinho, Regue and finally finishing in Porto again. Here we were travelling through the port country, some of the most beautiful parts of Portugal. The next year we took another river trip, this time on the Danube, visiting Bucharest, Vidin in Bulgaria, Belgrade in Serbia, travelling through Croatia, finishing in the beautiful city of Budapest in Hungary. So we have discovered yet another way of messing about in boats.

Golf

"Golf is an ideal diversion, but a ruinous disease."

B.C. Forbes (founder of *Forbes* magazine, 1880–1954)

Golf is not a sport but a punishment. I spent a considerable part of my life failing entirely to master the game. It begins when you're young and you are taken to putting greens in town parks or at seaside resorts. From here you graduate to Crazy Golf, a version that is remarkably like the real thing and should represent a warning. Then you move on to pitch and putt, which firmly engrains appalling habits that you will never eradicate from your game. And finally, you feel ready to tackle the championship course.

At this point you must have taken leave of your senses, but the cunning in the game is that some of the time you seem to play quite well, and you think, if I could practise a bit more ..., but you never do. It is an illusion. Your true game is all that slicing and hooking, topping and sclaffing, yes, and airshots.

My father played every Sunday morning for many years and never got below his official 24 handicap. I caddied for him once, to help break in a pair of hiking boots before a school camp, and saw that he was the weakest player. Years later, when my brother and I also played, the three of us were about as bad as each other and gave each other a close game.

The handicapping system is designed to allow the ordinary club player to compete with a scratch golfer. But it doesn't. To get a handicap you submit a number of cards in medal play. Most club players don't play this way. They usually play some variation that allows them to keep an interest. Medal play means that they will have been knocked out of the contest early on. I never played with an ordinary club member who played to his handicap. Usually they were scoring a lot more and you wondered how they had ever achieved a handicap. Occasionally they played below it. These were the cheats. All golfers cheat but some are more systematic. Most improve their lie, or need to be reminded of the extra shot in the woods, but there are a few who do it in a calculated way so that they can win invitational events on strange courses.

I never achieved a handicap and could not have sustained one. If asked what my handicap was I would always say, "My swing!" But I did play some of the great courses. I have played at over sixty courses over twenty years. In the UK these included Ferndown in Dorset; St Pierre in Chepstow; St Andrews (the New Course); The Belfry; Woburn (the Duke's Course); Foxhills, where I was a member; and the Royal Berkshire.

Abroad I have played in some spectacular places: Mijas on the Costa Del Sol within weeks of it opening; Mount Kenya safari park; the Reef Hotel, Seychelles, where a sign commands you to beware of falling coconuts; Hazeltine in Minnesota, where Tony Jacklin won his US Open; Sport Frances, where I was a member, Club de Polo and Prince of Wales (all in Santiago, Chile); Penina in the Algarve; Tropicana in Las Vegas; Belmont in Bermuda; Desert Dunes in Palm Springs; Le Saint Geran in Mauritius; Boca Raton in Florida; Kapalua in Maui; Glenoaks in Japan.

Glenoaks is a fantastic course where the Morita family has memberships. I was invited to play one Sunday while in Tokyo on a business trip with two Japanese and Gerry Ten Velden from Sony Holland. The course had a track for an automatic caddy car operated by a single female caddy of indeterminate age. While we walked and played she would control the cart remotely and run to fetch our clubs. She had a few words of English and would run after the ball on the green instructing it to "Stoppo!" My game was particularly desperate but with great sympathy she came up to me and suggested, "Mr Pearson. Change club?"

The key to understanding golf is to accept that it is impossible. Unlike most ball games the ball is stationary when you address it. You play your own ball, not that of your opponent. There is no reason, therefore, why the ball will not do exactly what you ask it to. In this respect it most closely resembles snooker. But this is another impossible game. Only a few poor souls who do nothing else in life begin to approach mastery in snooker.

You can always spot them from their sallow skin, as they never see the light of day. At least in golf you go outside and get some fresh air. But that is what you hit, most of the time: fresh air.

It helps, they say, if you have lessons, but this is not my experience. I studiously avoided lessons for years until we went to Corfu for a golfing holiday which was to include some time with a professional. There was a mix-up and the pro had different ideas but we persuaded him to give us one lesson. He asked me to hit a nine iron. I hit a straight ball about 150 yards and admired my handiwork. He said, "I bet you have trouble with your woods!" In one minute he had destroyed any remaining idea that I could play this game.

Sony Golf Day, September 1990. Cranfield Golf Club, DP with Tommy Horton.

In Chile, where I at least had predictable weather and could plan a weekend golf game, I took a course of lessons from a marvellous old teaching pro from Florida called Ace Noonan. Ace had come to Chile with the ambition of teaching someone to teach. He asked me to hit a nine iron. (Why do they all do that?) Again I hit it straight and he said that I was like the guy who goes to the doctor saying that he had a cold and the doctor would say, "Yes! And you have broken both of your legs!"

Ace set about rebuilding every part of my game. Stance, grip and swing were all analysed and explained. At first I did well as I concentrated on these new techniques, but then the old habits returned and I was more confused than ever. I now vacillated between the two styles and my game was even worse than before. I think that this is what all teaching pros are trying to do. They are like the drug dealer who innocently introduces you to something quite harmless and then takes you down a painful road of addiction. In golf you start with a few lessons, then a few more, then a new type of driver, then some new clothes and so it goes on.

On a return trip to Chile I arranged to play with my old golfing partner, Jim Callahan, at my old club, Sport Frances. Unfortunately Jim cancelled so Coca kindly offered to walk round with me. The caddies insisted that she should play and with instruction from her caddie she did very well. I was having a terrible round until the long 17th where I hit a splendid shot off the tee right down the middle of the fairway. My adrenaline was pumping so hard I couldn't wait to hit my second shot and marched after the ball leaving the caddie in my wake. Finally he reached me and I grabbed at the 4-iron. It shot up in the air and came down on my head. Not put off I hit the ball onto the green, a par five green in two with a chance of an eagle. My caddie said, "Señor should hit himself over the head more often!"

Mars gave me country club membership in Chile and Sony did the same later in my career when Nobu Watanabe returned to Japan. Haydn Abbott was promoted to Nobu's position and I think Nobu's way of expressing his confidence in me was to allocate one of the memberships at Foxhills. He had six, all of which were previously allocated to the Japanese expatriates. His one condition was that I use it to entertain. I tried but it was quite difficult to find customers as bad as me. Usually I preferred to play with staff members, many of whom were glad of a round on a great course. I often used it to explain a new idea in a different environment.

Gradually the Japanese returned home and when the memberships came up for renewal I cancelled them. I switched mine to the RAC which had a course nearer to our home in Reigate. There was a waiting list and my membership came through, but I had failed to understand that there was a separate waiting list for golf membership and so I was without a place to play. The final indignity came when Shin Takagi handed over to me as Managing Director of Sony United Kingdom. There was one remaining corporate membership which went with this job and that was at Wentworth. However, playing privileges were reserved for proper golfers and you had to play a round with the captain to qualify. I could not face that so I was a non-playing member of Wentworth for my last years with Sony.

But I got the last laugh. By now I had just about hung up my clubs. I last played in 1995. I would never say that I had given it up but the longer

I went without playing I knew that the harder it would be to return, and frankly, I did not really miss it. But I was still a member of the RAC, in my own name, and when the Club sold the Rescue Service I was one of the members who received the magnificent windfall of £32,500. I had finally won something at golf.

Reading (and Writing)

"The love of learning, the sequestered nooks,
And all the sweet serenity of books."

Henry Wadsworth Longfellow

Everyone says that one of their interests is reading but if you ask them in a job interview to tell you what they are reading now, most cannot do it. I always can – in fact, I'm usually reading two books, one fiction and one non-fiction. Currently I'm reading a John Grisham novel and a book about the connections between Great Britain and Chile in 1806–1831. I also have an audio book on the go, a travel story based on a trip to Baghdad.

My mother encouraged me to read. I was a regular user of the library from a very young age and she introduced me to many of my favourite writers. Our house wasn't overflowing with books but there was a good collection, including a full set of Reprint Society novels that my parents must have subscribed to.

We were allowed one comic each – this was the politically correct *Robin*, then *Swift*, and then I started to express my individualism by taking *Tiger*, which allowed me to read "Roy of the Rovers", purportedly written by my first football hero, Bobby Charlton. When I introduced a second comic into the house, *Victor*, my mother scolded me and banned it. That, of course, drove that habit underground and later I experimented with Superman comics and *Mad* magazine. She also disapproved when I exchanged a birthday gift token for a Famous Five novel. She was quite right; this was a waste of a chance to buy something more durable than a once-read-thrown-away children's thriller. I now think that all reading is good as long as some of it is stretching you in some way, either by making you think, or by teaching you new ideas or facts. But I have to confess I have read a lot of rubbish in my time.

At Manchester Grammar School I won two prizes, one in the first year and one on leaving. In the first year, with my mother's coaching, I won the Procter prize for reading, i.e. reading aloud. The prize was of course a book, but to a modest value. I took a biography of Sir Donald Bradman, another sporting hero. I still have this trophy. On leaving, I was awarded the Annie Burton Memorial Scholarship. I never discovered who Annie Burton was but this allowed me to put together a much more impressive list of books, including a dictionary of quotations and the complete works of Shakespeare and Marlowe.

I discovered two of my favourite authors about the same time. Sir Arthur Conan Doyle tried hard to be taken seriously for his literary works but his Sherlock Holmes stories are immortal and are easily the most enjoyable books to re-read that I have ever come across. They just outdistance the comic masterpieces of P.G. Wodehouse if only because there is a touch of repetition in Wodehouse – he sometimes struggles for a plot, even resorting to recycling his plot ideas, or even buying one on the open market, while Doyle seemed to have endless powers of invention. So Doyle gets my Desert Island vote and I would be happy to stay there on the island re-reading them until I had been able to write my own contribution to the canon. (Actually I did try this in one of our Christmas Newsletters as well as one inspired by the Jeeves stories.)

In the autumn of 1966, post A-levels, most MGS boys stayed on to enter the Oxbridge entrance exams held at the end of that term. I found this one of the most intensely satisfying intellectual periods of my education. Freed from the restrictions of the GCE syllabus I read over sixty books – novels, history, philosophy – in a period of just three months. From the earlier frivolity of comics and undemanding entertainment, at sixteen I was taking on modern classics as well as developing my ideas. Even so it was a shock to me that I passed the exam and gained a place at Oxford.

This next few years, first at Blake and then at New College, exposed me to people of similar intelligence and different backgrounds, and more rewarding than formal reading lists were the recommendations of a whole series of new friends. I discovered Dostoyevsky and Tolkien, Fowles and Ferlinghetti, Graves and Galsworthy this way.

But then on my leaving Oxford and taking up a business career, colleagues provided a different kind of stimulus, competitive rather than intellectual. Reading reverted to escapism and once more I scavenged among the trash. There were a few exceptions but I became a collector of the airport novel.

Giving up smoking provided a new stimulus. I took some time to give up, not just for the usual reasons of physical addiction but also because I did not want to replace one bad habit with another. So I resolved to use the money saved to buy books through a book club. For a number of years I took advantage of all the "join and you only have to buy three books" offers that came my way. I ruthlessly resigned from these clubs when I had fulfilled the minimum commitment and thus established the basis of a half-decent library.

I also rediscovered the ability to read a long book. As a boy I had devoured the works of Dumas even though they are exceptionally long novels, because they are so thrilling that the length is never an obstacle. Dickens had, however, been beyond me – perhaps we are introduced to such works too early. Now I could take on the long sagas of Clavell and Michener and later, with this ability, rediscovered the joys of Dickens, whose complete works I have now completed.

Fortunately, in Coca I found a kindred spirit. We shared interests in many things but especially reading and on our many holidays together she indulged my need to spend a considerable part of the holiday reading. She always made it a point to take at least one photo of me reading, as for her this captured part of the essence of our time together, and some of these are indescribably funny. One on the steps of the bus station in Zapallar in Chile shows me waiting for the bus but impervious to everything going on around me, and another shows me sitting on a sofa, wrapped up in a book, and surrounded by drying laundry of the most intimate nature.

A more recent and most welcome discovery has been the audio book. I count this as "reading" although strictly someone else is reading to you. To listen to Greta Scacchi reading Jane Austen or Timothy West reading the Flashman series is a great pleasure and, of course, extends the time for reading. I listen while walking or driving and I know others even use it as an aid to the ironing.

I now read between 50 and 100 books per year, much more than most I know, but a fraction of what Gladstone read. The GOM read some 20,000 books in his lifetime. Perhaps some were shorter than today's publications and no doubt it was a useful way to pass very long carriage journeys, but still it was a monumental achievement. I have probably read some 3,500 books so far and will never get near Mr Gladstone's figure.

But I won't stop trying.

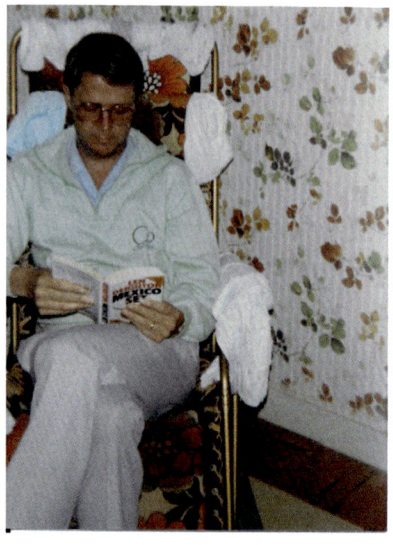

DP reading on holiday.

As for writing, again my mother set a good example. An inveterate letter writer and an enthusiastic diarist, she later took creative writing classes and was pleased with some of her efforts. My sister, Angela, is a fine writer and has contributed to published works on the Ethiopian famine and on other issues relating to aid to developing countries, as well as researching and writing a superb biography of her mother-in-law, Edith Penrose.

To date I have published two books. (This will be the third.) *The 20 Ps of Marketing* extends the original idea of the Four Ps of Marketing. It was published in 2013 and has been translated into Spanish and Chinese. *Marketing for Good is Good Marketing* is a compilation of the blogs I wrote during my year as Master of the Worshipful Company of Marketors.

I started writing my blogs in 2009 as a way of driving traffic to my website, www.davidcpearson.co.uk, which itself was designed to market me as an adviser. However, the blogs have taken on a life of their own. To date I have published over 500 with a total word count of over 750,000 words.

David Pearson

These few pages are my efforts to record something of my life, perhaps to amuse my family and friends when I am no longer here or at least no longer able to recall. Hemingway spoke of the fact that old men forget and so it is imperative to record when it remains fresh in the memory. I am not in Hemingway's class but can still follow his advice.

Walking

"... in the distant woods or fields, in unpretending sprout-lands or pastures tracked by rabbits, even in a bleak and, to most, cheerless day, like this, when a villager would be thinking of his inn, I come to myself, I once more feel myself grandly related, and that cold and solitude are friends of mine. I suppose that this value, in my case, is equivalent to what others get by churchgoing and prayer. I come home to my solitary woodland walk as the homesick go home. I thus dispose of the superfluous and see things as they are, grand and beautiful. I have told many that I walk every day about half the daylight, but I think they do not believe it. I wish to get the Concord, the Massachusetts, the America, out of my head and be sane a part of every day."

Thoreau's Journal, 7th January 1857

All of us learn to walk at about the age of 1 and then some of us learn to walk again, in my case at about the age of 11. I was lucky enough to attend a school with a fine walking tradition. Camps were held in the Lake District to introduce boys to the character-building traditions of camping in the wettest valleys in England. To escape from these valleys involved walking, including climbs up steep passes to local mountain tops. I found all this exciting and invigorating. Even as a boy who had most of his growing in front of him, I would dog the footsteps of the master who led the walk and then, once allowed, race with a handful of others to be the first to the summit.

Threads and Patches

I attended three Borrowdale camps with MGS in the Whitsun holidays of my first three years, as well as a less demanding camp one summer in Grasmere. All of these gave me a love of mountains and lakes, the challenge of the climb with its false summits and the intense satisfaction of gaining the top.

With this experience I was able to gravitate to the more demanding treks organised by the school. While the camps were in fixed locations, on trek we carried our gear from site to site. Ian "Basher" Bailey, one of the most charismatic masters in the school, enthused us with the attractions of Scottish Trek, which he led. He taught me English in my second year and History in my fourth and used a substantial part of teaching time to apprise us of the progress he was making in negotiating routes across the great landowners' estates in the wildest parts of Scotland.

In the summer of 1965 as an immature 15-year-old sixth former I joined Scottish Trek, which had the particularly attractive route of the Western Highlands via Fort William and Ben Nevis, then across to the Isle of Skye and back to Mallaig in time to see the Highland Games there. It was a wonderful experience and an important rite of passage.

The following summer I joined Foreign Trek, which had the even more ambitious and attractive target of circumnavigating Mont Blanc, the highest mountain in Europe at 4,810m above sea level. This would take us through three countries, France, Switzerland and Italy, and was my first experience of travel abroad. We travelled by train across France, through Paris and then down to the mountains near the Swiss border. We took the clockwise route around Mont Blanc finishing in Chamonix.

At each site we would pitch camp for a few days and as well as occasional rest days, take so-called excursions up to higher points without our camping gear. Our party was about forty-five strong including four masters and I suppose we all took it on trust that they had the experience to lead us.

On one excursion I had my doubts. From a site in Courmayeur at 1,224m in Northern Italy, we planned to climb up to the Rifugio Nuovo Torino (Mount Blanc) at a height of 3,382m above sea level, well above the snow line even in high summer. We had no climbing equipment but as we climbed up to the summit it was clear that our masters, "Artie" Khan and Brian Phythian, were unsure about proceeding. I was as always near

Rifugio Nuovo Torino, (Mont Blanc).

the front and I was glad of it because there were many loose rocks, and some of these were dislodged and went hurtling down past the heads of those below.

Finally we made the summit and it was decided to descend by cable car rather than risk the downward descent on the difficult surface. We had ascended more than 2,000 metres, a greater climb than is possible in any part of the United Kingdom from sea level to the highest mountain tops, but taking risks that today would be completely ruled out under health and safety legislation.

To emphasise the dangers, while our school party was trekking round Mont Blanc, Richard Harris, my first-year form master, was part of a separate group making an attempt on the summit. Unfortunately, bad weather overcame them and all of the party lost their lives.

Less dangerous but still with plenty of exposure to the elements were two hikes I undertook with the Senior Scouts. As part of gaining one's First Class badge it was necessary to take a two-day hike following map directions that were sealed until the hike began. Two Scouts were to travel together, neither of whom had passed the badge. Neil Culliford was ahead of me and invited me to accompany him. The hike was in a tough part of the Peak District and involved a very cold night at the head of the Goyt Valley. The following day the farmer's red setter followed us. After some miles we realised he had adopted us for good and finally we had to return him via the local police station. Whether distracted by the dog, or the cold, or just by our own inadequacies, Neil failed the test so when it was my turn some weeks later I asked him to join me.

I had contracted a cold after our first effort so resolved to be better prepared. The scouting manuals talked of collecting dry firewood from the centre of hedgerows and then warming it in the oven. I took this too literally and lit the oven, which of course quickly set the wood on fire. My long-suffering parents cleared up the mess and amazingly still allowed me to go on my hike. In retrospect, I should have been failed at that point.

I collected my map directions and as it was now late autumn we did not have to negotiate the heights of the Peak District but the lowlands of the Cheshire plain. What the planner had not taken into account is that the M6 had by now been built across this plain and so we had to find foot bridges across this in both directions, thus extending our hike enormously. Perhaps it was because of this that I was deemed to have passed and so became a First Class Scout!

The highest mountain I have climbed is El Teide in Tenerife. This is the third largest volcano on earth. Like Mauna Loa and Mauna Kea (the first- and second-largest volcanoes), Teide is a shield volcano. Elevation at the summit of the volcano is 12,188 feet (3,715 m). My climb was not as great as when we reached the Rifugio Nuovo Torino (Mount Blanc) as

El Teide, Tenerife.

it started with a coach trip that took us to a near point, but we still climbed the last 500 metres or so and many people found the effort too great as at that height oxygen starts to be thinner and even healthy people may not be able to manage it. Back in 1977 I managed this without difficulty but I suspect it would not be so easy today.

These days my walks are less ambitious but no less vital. Walking has become my most important form of exercise having displaced golf (I'm no good and it's not aerobic), tennis (ditto), squash (certainly aerobic but you need to be fit to play squash, not play squash to get fit), and the gym (certainly aerobic but boring and expensive). Walking is virtually free although I do use a gallon of petrol to explore new walks. Over the past thirty-five years or so I have explored large areas of Surrey, Kent, Hertfordshire, Buckinghamshire and Bedfordshire. One of the great strengths of England is the fantastic network of historic rights of way, well maintained as footpaths and bridleways. I mark these on my maps and have a spider's web of markings. In this way, while only walking six or so miles at a time, I sometimes complete long-established routes in an eclectic manner.

On the way I usually listen to music or sport on the radio or to one of my talking books. This doubles the pleasure and gives me marvellous exercise in the fresh air with great views of the English countryside, listening to entertainment.

Every Boxing Day I used to go on The Boxing Day Run with Andy Mills-Baker, a former neighbour. In our case this was a walk but it was livened up by the setting of cryptic clues to be solved at various map references. Over several years our best performance was third which, given our handicap as walkers competing with runners a generation younger, is not bad but in 2008 we won it by getting all the questions right. The organisers marked us down on one question because they said we couldn't get 100 per cent.

Tennis

I am useless at tennis. I even had a course of lessons when we lived in Reigate but it made no difference. I was quite good at table tennis and played on a number of representative teams, but lawn tennis, forget it.

But I do enjoy watching some professional tennis. I have been to Wimbledon several times and even saw some of the Italian Open in Rome when I was head of Ellesse, which had several sponsorship relationships in tennis.

I first went to Wimbledon as a student in my Oxford days. With a friend we just pitched up on the day and were able to get in, not to Centre Court, of course, but there's plenty of good tennis on the outside courts. In 1971 we saw Margaret Court and Evonne Goolagong, probably Australia's best ever women tennis players. I had previously only watched Wimbledon on television, black and white back then. The cameras are at one end because to film from the side would make you nauseous. But this has the effect of foreshortening the play. Watching from the side I was amazed how fast it is.

Sony had a close relationship with Wimbledon as the company supplied and maintained much of the broadcast equipment, so we had no problem booking tickets on the Show Courts and entertaining our customers and their spouses, firstly in a marquee for lunch and then on the courts. In my first year in 1989 I went on three days in the second week and saw Martina Navratilova, John McEnroe, Stefan Edberg, Mats Wilander and Ivan Lendl, among other fine players. Navratilova and Edberg were both losing finalists that year. In 1990 I just attended one day but saw Steffi Graf and Jana Novotná play in the quarter-final. Graf was defending champion but lost in the semi-final to Zina Garrison, who in turn lost to Navratilova in the final. I attended one day in 1991 but my records don't say whom I saw, but in 1992 I saw McEnroe again, this year unseeded, knock out the No. 16 seed David Wheaton in the third round. In 1993 I watched Boris Becker beat Henri Leconte and Andre Agassi beat Richard Krajicek in the fourth round. Agassi lost to that year's champion Pete Sampras in the quarter-final and Becker also lost to Sampras in the semi-final. In 1994 I saw three third-round matches, one of which featured the charismatic Goran Ivanišević, who went on to lose in the final to Sampras.

Pat Rafter at the Italian Open in 1999.

That was the last year that Sony gave this particular kind of hospitality.

I was lucky enough to go to Wimbledon in 1997 where I watched Pete Sampras win through to another final by beating Todd Woodbridge in the semi-final. Sampras went on to win his fourth of six Wimbledon titles. Woodbridge was better known as a doubles player and that year won his sixth Wimbledon doubles championship with Mark Woodforde.

The following year I left Sony and joined Pentland, a major sportswear brand owner. One of my brands was Ellesse which had been founded in Italy as both a skiing and a tennis brand. I was invited to watch some men's quarter-finals of the Italian Open in Rome and among others saw the great Australian Pat Rafter. This was the first and only time I've watched tennis played on clay and was fascinated by the way an umpire could make a call by checking the pitch mark of the ball.

There was then quite a gap before one of my clients at Critical Eye, Bill Payne of IBM, invited me and Coca as his guests. IBM by now had developed a strong commercial relationship with Wimbledon and had a permanent luxurious hospitality suite. In 2012 we saw the Spaniard David Ferrer, No. 7 seed, beat Juan Martin Del Potro, No. 9 seed. Ferrer would lose to Andy Murray, 4th seed that year, in the quarter-final. Murray lost the final to Roger Federer. We also saw Serena Williams beat the No. 4 seed Petra Kvitová in the fourth round on her way to winning the title for the fifth time. The following year, as Bill's guests, we again saw Kvitová, seeded 8th, lose this time to the German Kirsten Flipkens, seeded 20th. Flipkens got through to the semi-final where she went out to the Italian Marion Bartoli, seeded 15. We also saw the Polish No. 4 seed Agnieszka Radwańska beat the Chinese No. 6 seed Li Na. Radwańska lost in the semi-final to the German No. 23 seed Sabine Lisiecki, who in an earlier round had knocked out the defending champion and No. 1 seed Serena Williams. Bartoli beat Lisiecki in the final.

So in all I have watched tennis at ten major tournaments and seen some of the best players of the time. Sampras and Navratilova were no doubt the best I saw but my personal favourite was Stefan Edberg, who had a style and a crispness to his serve-and-volley game that particularly appealed to me.

Part IV
Reflections and Observations

My Blogs

In this part of the book I am going to include a selected number of the nearly 500 blogs I have published on my personal website, www.davidcpearson.co.uk, since 2009. I began these with the purpose of driving traffic to my website where I used to promote my services as a Non-Executive Chairman or Director or Adviser. But over the years they have taken on a life of their own; I have a large following and many of my readers correspond with me, sharing their own reflections and observations. In some cases this has probably prolonged and strengthened friendships that might otherwise have lapsed.

The great majority are on business or current affairs or big issues like climate change and sustainability, about which I feel strongly. But they don't belong in a book like this, which is intended more as a celebration of life rather than a rant about what's going wrong. I could easily fill several books with that stuff. No, instead I will concentrate on the more idiosyncratic and personal reflections and observations I have made. I will date them and reproduce them as they were published rather than re-edit them. I will group them by major theme.

History

Manchester Grammar School at 500

25th July 2015

Last week I attended a service in Exeter Cathedral to honour the founder of Manchester Grammar School, Hugh Oldham, Bishop of Exeter. The service is held every year but this year marked the 500th anniversary of the foundation of the school in 1515. I recall the 450th anniversary of the school when I was in the 6th form and Her Majesty Queen Elizabeth II visited the school to mark the occasion. That was in the days when the school was the largest and probably the most famous of the Direct Grant Grammar Schools, so it was possibly seen as appropriate for the sovereign to grace us with her presence. In that year, 1965, 65 per cent of the boys in the school had their fees paid directly by the state or by local authorities. The remaining 35 per cent paid full or partial fees based on the assessment of parental income. In my case I received a full scholarship paid by Cheshire Local Education Authority. These days the school is independent and so not even one of the minor royals is coming to mark the occasion.

It is worth trying to understand how we got to where we are now with a divided system of state and private schools. The earliest schools were founded by the Church. The first was King's Canterbury in 597, but although new schools were to appear over the course of the next eight hundred years, they were still very few in number. Then in the late 14th and 15th centuries, schools that were independent of the Church started to appear. Eton and Winchester are probably the best known of these.

Eton College was founded in 1440 by King Henry VI to provide free education for seventy poor boys who would then go on to King's College, Cambridge, founded by the same king in 1441. He took Winchester as his model, which was founded in 1382 by William of Wykeham, Bishop of Winchester, who was also Chancellor to both Edward III and Richard II. He had also founded New College, Oxford in 1379, my other alma mater, to which Winchester would act as a feeder. The first seventy poor scholars attended Winchester in 1394.

What followed in the next two hundred years was a huge growth of similar schools, usually founded by wealthy benefactors to enable the education of those from poor or disadvantaged backgrounds. It was in this environment that Hugh Oldham founded MGS, the first school in Manchester, with a mission to educate the best boys in the region, regardless of background. The Founder's Statutes state:

"there shall be no scollar or infaunt, of what country or
shire soever he be of, beyng man-child, be refused."

That mission was fulfilled throughout its history although over time, all these schools started to take on fee-paying pupils as well as scholarship students. The original foundations were, on the whole, only sufficient to provide a very basic education to a small number of pupils. Gradually the income from fees exceeded the value of the foundation income and the concept of the modern fee-paying private school emerged.

In the 1944 Education Act, designed by Conservative minister R.A. Butler, the idea of the Direct Grant Grammar school was introduced to open up a group of what were by then elite private schools to pupils from poorer backgrounds. MGS was one of 179 schools that signed up to the system whereby the state funded a quarter of all places and a further quarter could be funded at the discretion of the local authorities. The remaining places would be for fee payers.

The scheme lasted for a mere thirty years, but this is generally recognised as the period where any individual boy or girl had the best chances of being socially mobile. There were undoubtedly "losers" in the system too as another idea launched in the 1944 Act, the vocational school which would teach useful skills, largely failed to materialise and the majority, perhaps as many as 80 per cent who 'failed' the 11+, examination went to secondary modern schools, which they would leave at 14 or 15. But during that period a generation of politicians, lawyers, doctors and businessmen included boys from council estates as well as those from the middle and upper classes. As we all wore the same uniform I had no idea of a form mate's background until he invited me to his home for a birthday party or weekend stay.

The loss of the direct grant began in 1975 and schools had to choose between joining the maintained sector as comprehensives or going independent. Of the 179 schools about a quarter joined the state sector, nearly all of these being Catholic schools. The remainder became independent and include the likes of MGS, Leeds and Bradford Grammars and King Edward's Birmingham, in short some of the most successful schools in England.

In an attempt to ensure that students from poor backgrounds still had access to a place at the leading schools, there was a brief stay of execution in the form of the Assisted Places Scheme, set up by the Conservatives in 1980 but abolished by Tony Blair's government in 1997 as one of its first acts. It is ironic in this short history that every action to increase social mobility has been by Conservatives and every action to kill it has been by Labour.

Once state funding was removed, schools that were formerly drivers of mobility became the preserve of those who could afford the fees. (See my blog "Social Mobility in Education", 25th February 2012, https://davidcpearson.co.uk/blog.cfm?blogID=182.) These private schools are run to such a high standard that they are much in demand. Consequently they have been able to increase their fees much faster than inflation and so over the past twenty years or so the intake has changed beyond recognition. To attend a London day school parents have to have £20,000 of disposable income per child. If you want boarding that rises to about £34,000. The top boarding schools now compete in a global market and offer the special character of an English education to the children of the world's mega rich.

This has led to an unhealthy debate about the private schools with a strong flavour of class warfare. The fact that so many of the Cabinet were educated at famous public schools fuels the debate. When the current

Prime Minister, Archbishop of Canterbury and Mayor of London all went to Eton, reasoned debate starts to go out the window. Some figures are quoted but largely in a meaningless way. This comes from the *New Statesman*:

> While private schools only educate 7 per cent of the population, their students take up almost half the places at Oxbridge and one-third of the places across the whole Russell Group.

What the writers forget is that in the 1960s, when I went to Oxford, about half my fellow students came from the grammar schools. It was left-wing dogma that drove these schools into the private sector. The article goes on to say:

> We need to look closely at the facts. As one examines the figures for the 1200 member schools of the Independent Schools Council, a few things become clear: although 33.7 per cent of pupils at private schools receive help with their fees, two-thirds of these are either reductions for military, clergy, siblings and staff, or scholarships, and generally they provide only a quarter of the average day fee; only one in twelve private school students receives a means-tested bursary; and among these, 58.6 per cent are still paying at least half the fee. The number of students in receipt of a full bursary, paying no fees at all, is fewer than one in a hundred.

Dr Martin Boulton is the current high master of MGS. He benefited from the Assisted Places Scheme as a scholarship boy at the school in the 1980s, one of the last generation to have his social mobility funded by the state. He argues that the analysis of the *New Statesman* is essentially meaningless. The issue is about access. This was recognised by his predecessor Dr Martin Stephen, who set about raising funds to refound the school in the 1990s. He set a target of £20 million. To date £25 million has been raised, mostly from Old Boys. MGS is currently giving bursaries to 212 boys. The average means-tested bursary supports 92 per cent of the fees, all made possible by the generosity of the Old Boys. It seems that

MGS is the only school to have done this in this way, though there is great interest in how it has been achieved, particularly from other former Direct Grant Schools.

Having seen what can be done in just a couple of decades, Dr Boulton wants to get back to the point where MGS was as a Direct Grant Grammar School and to continue that in perpetuity. He calculates that would require something in the region of £75m to £100m. In the early 16th century the school was founded by visionary and wealthy founders. Every day in assembly we said a prayer in thanks to this group of men and women, eleven of whom are named in the prayer. In 1931 the school needed to raise a sum to move its premises from a then over-crowded site in the centre of Manchester to a much larger site in its own grounds, where it still stands a few miles out in Rusholme. This was in the depth of the depression but I have in my possession a copy of the building appeal for £150,000. This was led by many eminent citizens of the city and their subscriptions are listed, including two of £1,000, equivalent to perhaps £60,000 today. If they could do it then, surely we can do it now and refound the school for the next 500 years.

Politics and Economics
Small States

24th February 2018

My wife and I have just returned from holiday in the United Arab Emirates. We visited five of the seven Emirates, staying in four. Our purpose was primarily sun and sand rather than culture and history, but it is difficult not to be impressed with their success in creating an international business cluster in the desert.

The United Arab Emirates used to be the Trucial States, protectorates but not colonies of the British Empire. In 1958 Abu Dhabi discovered oil, followed by Dubai in 1966. Abu Dhabi's reserves proved immense and still account for 89 per cent of its economy. Dubai's were more modest, now accounting for only 5 per cent, and perhaps its progress is more remarkable as its leaders realised early that limited and relatively modest reserves would not guarantee long-lasting wealth unless some of their proceeds were reinvested in sustainable businesses.

So, somewhat like Norway used its North Sea Oil to create the largest sovereign wealth fund in the world, Dubai has become a regional leader in many business circles. What these states have in common is that they are comparatively small, that is in their native population. Their GDP is minor in world terms, but their GDP per capita is world leading. And that is why they can make such strong progress, at least in economic terms, though arguably in many other fields as well.

Again this week I heard some clown on the radio describing Britain as rich because it was a member of the G8 and should therefore have outstanding public services and infrastructure. Britain is not rich in GDP per capita terms and squandered its North Sea windfall on revenue accounts, rather than capital expenditure. Its Imperial history means it feels it must maintain the trappings of a powerful country with nuclear weapons, a space programme and so on. But such expenditure means that there is not enough for public services and infrastructure. The problems of being large countries also affect the newcomers on the world stage. China and India also have their nuclear weapons and their space programmes even though both countries are extremely poor in GDP per capita terms.

The top ten countries ranked by nominal GDP per capita are:

1. Luxembourg
2. Switzerland
3. Norway
4. Iceland
5. Ireland
6. Qatar
7. United States
8. Denmark
9. Australia
10. Singapore

Of these only the United States could really be described as large. All the rest have populations of below 20 million; most well below. The United Kingdom comes in at 22nd. The United Arab Emirates is 24th but this covers the poorer Emirates with no oil as well as Abu Dhabi and Dubai. It also includes the large immigrant population which is not permanent but mainly migrant workers. When only the Emirati are considered they rocket up the table. China is 72nd, below Kazakhstan and above Nauru. India does not appear on this list, which is the latest from the IMF for 2017, but on the United Nations List is 144th, sandwiched between São Tomé and Principe, and Moldova.

GDP per capita is sometimes taken as a measure of the general standard of living. This is clearly rubbish as these big powerful states use much of their GDP on their vanity projects at the expense of the general standard of living. There is no doubt that millions have been lifted out of poverty in

China and India but there is also no doubt that many more millions remain in abject poverty.

Britain also suffers in this league table because of its excess centralisation of power and economic activity. Its regions are mainly much poorer. Germany by contrast has little centralisation. Its business and cultural centres are well distributed. While parts of Britain seek independence there is little evidence that they would benefit from this. At present under the Barnett formula there are vast transfers of money from the centre to the regions, particularly Scotland. These would cease if Scotland were to leave the UK.

But in other parts of Europe it might be a different story. One of the reasons for the failure of the EU is it restricts the natural growth of its smaller members. They are trapped in a web of protectionism and idiotic monetary policy that prevents them from growing. The recent moves in Catalonia for independence have been very clumsily managed by both sides politically, but if it were more intelligently managed it could lead to significant economic advancement. So far the Catalan secession makes Brexit look well planned.

But if this were looked at differently it could be the way forward for much of Europe. Note that in the list above, the top five are all European small states, three in the EU and the other two in well-developed trade agreements with the EU. But the larger EU nations are all well down the table: Germany 17th, France 21st, UK 22nd, Italy 25th and Spain 27th. And just to be clear, GDP per capita in Luxembourg is four times that of Spain.

If Europe were based on more powerful regions, and perhaps more nations as well, it could be much more successful. The EU has been centralising power for several decades now and there is not much to show for it. These regions are already among the richest: Catalonia in Spain; Bavaria in Germany; Lombardy and Veneto in Italy. With goodwill and flexibility in providing access to markets rather than the bad will and revolting protectionism of today's EU, such secessions could benefit everyone.

Lots of smaller states would also encourage diversity, innovation, competition and more experimentation. It is not a coincidence that the richest countries in terms of GDP per capita are all small. Their leaders can focus on the issues that matter to them. Look around the world at the big countries and they are all ungovernable unless autocratic measures are used, as in China and Russia.

I started by showing how natural resources had been used in Dubai and Norway to promote wider economic growth. But Luxembourg, Switzerland and Singapore had no such advantages. Some countries in the world complain that they are land-locked and demand access to the sea. Luxembourg and Switzerland are land-locked, have few natural resources and are the two richest countries in the world in GDP per capita. What they are very good at is focusing on industries where they are strong, building great trading relationships, and creating the kind of deregulated, low-tax, free trading economies that are well suited to the 21st century. In a small country it is easier to unite behind a single goal. In big countries the politicians cannot make decisions and therefore do not progress. They fundamentally get in the way.

Matthew Lynn, distinguished financial commentator, put it this way:

> Europe has had half a century of progressively centralising power, and the results have hardly been impressive. It's been stuck with a moribund economy, mass unemployment, and a dysfunctional currency. It is hard to see how regions splintering away could make it much worse, and they might make it a lot better – by allowing more cohesive states to emerge, and new policies to be tried out.

> "Europe should let its regions break free",
> Matthew Lynn, *MoneyWeek*, 3rd November 2017

Current Affairs
Smoked Salmon

28th July 2018

My wife and I recently visited H. Forman & Son, home of the world famous "London Cure" smoked Scottish salmon, a true gourmet food with protected status. The Forman family has been curing and smoking fish in the East End of London since 1905. Today the smokehouse produces H. Forman & Son specialities for leading food retailers and their chefs create top quality restaurant dishes – fish, meat and vegetarian – for hotels and fine-dining establishments across the world.

We toured part of the smokehouse and saw a live demonstration of slicing fresh smoked salmon by the holder of the Guinness World Record for this skill. Forman's are passionate about their London Cured smoked salmon which they have been producing for four generations, so it was a proud day for them when their London Cure smoked salmon was recognised as a delicacy worthy of PGI certification – a protected food name status similar to Champagne, Roquefort, Parma ham, Melton Mowbray pork pies and Wensleydale cheese, to name just a few.

The present owner, Lance Forman, gave a fascinating talk about his family history – his great-grandfather came to England to escape the Russian pogroms and set up a business curing salmon as many of his fellow immigrants did in the East End. At first they continued to use Norwegian salmon which took several days to arrive by boat. Then they discovered the marvellous Scottish salmon which could get to London by train in less than a day.

Lance was educated at Cambridge University, where he became President of the Union, and before joining the family business qualified as an accountant with PwC (PricewaterhouseCoopers), advised the Rt Hon Peter Lilley MP when he was in the Cabinet, and developed some property interests when opportunities in Eastern Europe opened up. All of this was useful experience as the fortunes of the business were mixed. He nearly lost his factory to flood and then did lose it to fire. He rebuilt it to a higher standard but then he lost that to the might of the London Olympics.

This is not really a blog about smoked salmon but about how, far from the London Olympics being a force for regeneration, it was the exact opposite. It slowed down regeneration that was already taking place in the area and put hundreds of businesses out of business. That H. Forman & Sons survived is tribute to the remarkable fighting qualities and resilience of Lance, his family and his staff.

On 6th July 2005, the world held a collective breath as IOC President Jacques Rogge declared: 'The games of the 30th Olympiad in 2012 are awarded to the city of … London.' For many British this was cause for jubilation and literally dancing in the streets. For Forman's and its neighbouring businesses on the designated site it was a potential death sentence.

The area around Stratford was already a scene of thriving regeneration. The Stratford City project was going well. The high-speed rail links to Stratford International were in place. The industrial park that had been chosen as the principal site for the development of new stadia for a two-week sporting celebration was already the home of 350 local businesses employing 12,000 people. When the Games took place much was made of the 11,000 jobs created. But most of these were temporary volunteer jobs, while most of the 12,000 full-time jobs were destroyed forever.

In his remarkable book *Forman's Games* Lance Forman pulls no punches in an unexpurgated account about how he and his colleagues tried to deal with bullying and obfuscation, delaying tactics and sinister undercover dealings by the combined forces of the establishment, concerned with just the single object of putting on a show. In that they succeeded, but in the creation of a legacy that justified the enormous cost to the taxpayer and to individual businessmen, they almost totally failed.

The smoked salmon business is, of course, dealing with a perishable commodity. It literally receives many of its orders overnight from restaurant chefs who leave a message on an answerphone. When his factory burnt down Lance's main concern was to get hold of the answering machine so that he could still fulfil the overnight orders. The firemen barred his entrance but he insisted, and together with a brave member of staff retrieved the machine and saved at least the day's orders.

Forman's reputation with its customers is such that they might survive a day or two's missed production but not more. So when the London Development Authority unfairly acquired Compulsory Purchase Order powers to build the stadia, Lance's main concern was the lead time he would get to find a new convenient site and to build a new factory.

Compulsory Purchase Powers are not available to the government and its agencies just to build new entertainment facilities. They must be used for some higher purpose such as regeneration. And this is what the LDA used as its argument. But the regeneration was already going well. Lance surmises in the book that the LDA did not really want the London bid to succeed but were hoping that the Paris bid would win as indeed most commentators and the bookies all thought would happen. They underestimated the sales qualities of Tony Blair, Princess Anne, Sebastian Coe and David Beckham. They also underestimated the blundering of President Jacques Chirac who said the only food worse than the British was the Finnish. The Finns held one of the key casting votes as previously undecided, and promptly sided with London.

Once the Games were awarded to London the LDA had no choice but to swing into action and file a series of CPOs against 350 thriving businesses in the area. Lance tells how they did everything possible to delay and obfuscate, sometimes telling blatant untruths about the availability of alternative sites. Lance was effectively doing two jobs now: his normal job of trying to run a successful food business and the unwelcome but unavoidable one of dealing with a bunch of bureaucrats in his efforts to keep the business alive.

He needed a minimum of two years' notice to locate and build his new factory. Eventually after gargantuan efforts he succeeded in finding a location right next to the site of the new stadium across the river. His old factory was the last to be destroyed and the authorities insisted on sticking to a quite unreasonable deadline in Forman's' vacating the premises. Having stuck to the deadline, Lance was then mortified to see that no new action took place on his site for many weeks. As he developed his new site he saw many opportunities to use it to expand his business and create a hospitality venue and tourist destination. As the run up to the Games developed there were many who thought he was now sitting on a gold mine for potential extra business over the period of the Games.

But again the authorities frustrated every attempt to do this. He found that whatever he planned, the Olympic Games "police" would thwart him. Some of the Games volunteers, the so-called Games Makers, were enlisted to tear down all his promotional material.

Indeed this was the experience across London. The centre of London became a ghost town as restaurants closed their doors. Everyone had been put off by the warnings of the IOC about traffic and so on.

A very senior civil servant once told me that the initial costings of the Games had been hastily written "back-of-the-envelope" estimates. No one really thought that London would win. When Arup was commissioned to do an analysis of these costings they made it clear that they were inadequate and would need serious revision, but no such action took place.

One of my jobs involves regular visits to the Olympic site, now called Here East. There are a few operations there involving some inward investment but judging by the relatively few courtesy buses that I use to go from Stratford International to the office there are nothing like the number of workers there that were in the original plans used by Sebastian Coe and others to justify the investment and the so-called legacy.

Similarly, while it is not the thrust of Lance Forman's book, there has been no sporting legacy. No provision was made to prepare for the interest that British medal success in cycling and rowing might generate, so the facilities and the coaching were not there when excited youngsters turned up. They soon lost interest and went back to their video games rather than the real thing.

And my visit also taught me that there is a genuine difference in high-quality smoked salmon like Forman's as opposed to the banal offering by most of the supermarkets. Over decades their demands for lower prices have debased the product. In an attempt to restore some of its flavour or to overcome the problems created, most suppliers now add Demerara sugar.

Look it up on the label. There should be no added sugar in smoked salmon. It might cost you a bit more for the real thing but it's well worth it. And I can recommend a visit. Boris Johnson described it as the smoked salmon theme park.

Foreign Affairs
The Chilean Way

23rd October 2010

This is my 50th blog and I make no apologies in using the occasion to return to the subject of Chile, a land that I love. In this year of the bicentenary of her independence from Spain, Chile has been in the news for extraordinary reasons. Firstly the peaceful transfer of power from a centre-left coalition to a centre-right coalition led by Sebastián Piñera. Then, before he had taken over as President, an earthquake measured at 8.8 on the Richter scale, the fifth most powerful in recorded history. And most recently the amazing rescue of thirty-three miners from a cave nearly half a mile below the surface of the Atacama Desert.

President Piñera stayed at the pithead for 48 hours continuously without sleep to greet each of the miners and the rescue team as they emerged from the rescue capsule, and immediately after the rescue was complete flew to London on an official visit. His first engagement was a reception last Saturday at the Park Lane Hilton to which my wife and I were invited and where we had the chance to meet him. I felt privileged to be there as one of only a handful of Britons, as the event was intended for the Chilean community. After a spirited singing of the Chilean national anthem he told us the story of the rescue. He was informed of the accident when he was on a diplomatic visit to Ecuador. He and his Minister of Mining, Lawrence Golborne, immediately recognised that the private company which operated the mine was not capable of a rescue, which, if successful, would be the deepest rescue ever made anywhere in the world. The decision to take responsibility was not hard intellectually but was hard emotionally, but they made it that night. Then 17 days of exploratory drilling went on before contact was made with the famous piece of paper with the message. "We are safe in a refuge here, the 33." The President showed us the actual piece of paper that was received.

President Piñera greeting one of "The 33".
Photograph Ho/Reuters.

That day the President's father-in-law was dying and Piñera went to say goodbye to him. The old man's last words were "You must save them!" With such a message of encouragement his own formidable resolve was further strengthened. He instructed his Cabinet to seek whatever help was required anywhere in the world. Three different drilling attempts were made, one with American technology, one Australian and one Chilean. It was actually the Chilean drill that won. Then the rescue was prepared and much of the world watched it, an estimated audience of 1.2 billion. "Why," asked President Piñera, "did so many people follow a story of thirty-three miners at the end of the world?" The answer, he believed, was that this was a good-news story, and I think that's right even though we were aware of journalists here in London trying to find some political angle. My wife was asked by one journalist if the whole thing had been a put-up job to attract publicity.

What is true is that President Piñera has unashamedly taken the opportunity to try to change the way the world thinks about Chile. Rather than a country notorious for its military government (see my blog "Democracy in Chile", 23 January 2010, https://davidcpearson.co.uk/blog.cfm?blogID=70), she is a country united, hopeful and capable. Although the earthquake caused $30 billion of damage, 18 per cent of Chile's GDP, already more than 80 per cent of infrastructural damage has been repaired and the government has already achieved its targets of building emergency housing for the homeless, getting all children back to school and replacing most of the hospital beds lost.

On Monday President Piñera gave a lecture at the LSE to which we were also invited. He received a standing ovation from the packed audience, mainly of students even though I suspect most of the students there were left wing. Piñera told us that he plans to restore Chile's previous fast rates of growth, lost in the past few years, to 6 per cent per year and is on track to do that this year despite the earthquake. He wants to defeat poverty in the next decade and achieve social justice and equal opportunities for all. He will use the old pillars of democracy, economy and a strong state to fight excessive inequality but add to these the new pillars of human capital, investment, entrepreneurship, innovation and technology. He wants to create 1 million new jobs by 2014, 20 per cent of the labour force, and is on the way with 300k this year compared with just 30k in the last year of his predecessor.

He told us of the Chilean paradox. While spending just one-seventh of US rates of expenditure per head on health, Chilean life expectancy is equivalent, its cancer death rate far lower and its obesity rates a third. He plans to double public subsidies on education and lift the remaining 15 per cent of the population out of poverty.

President Piñera is a man in a hurry. Chilean presidents only have a single four-year term so he has a lot to do if he is going to achieve these and other ambitious objectives. But he has already had three successful careers, as a billionaire businessman, as an academic and as a politician. He was the son of a diplomat who was ambassador to Belgium and then the United Nations and so he grew up with an international outlook. He took his first degree in Chile and then his Masters and Doctorate in Harvard. At the age of 27 he returned to Chile having negotiated the rights to represent both MasterCard and Visa in Chile. That was the basis of his first fortune which he later diversified into a wide variety of interests, including ownership of 27 per cent of LanChile and Chilevision, Chile's 4th largest TV station. He has sold his interests in LanChile and Chilevision, but kept his 13 per cent holding of Colo Colo, a football club, because he wants to help them win the Copa Libertadores, the equivalent of the Champions' League in South America.

As a senator he was voted the best in the senate even though he was from a minority right-wing party. As President he has proved inclusive and accompanying him in the delegation to London were senators and deputies from all sides of the spectrum including Senator Letelier, son of Orlando Letelier, the former Ambassador to the United Nations and later activist against President Pinochet who was murdered by Pinochet's secret police on the streets of Washington DC in 1976.

For years the world has thought of events like that when they think of Chile. President Piñera wants to change all that. As he told Luis Alberto Urzua, the last miner out, who was the shift foreman credited with helping the trapped miners endure seventeen days in isolation before Chileans discovered the men had survived the mine collapse, "You are not the same, and the country is not the same after this."

Foreign Affairs

Third Man in Havana

11th August 2012

As the Super-Size Big-Mac Games waddles to its close, one of the world's most popular sports is conspicuous by its absence. While golf and rugby are going to return to the Summer Olympic schedule in 2016 this sport has only been contested once at the Games, in 1900. The reigning Olympic Champions are Great Britain while the silver medal was won by France (good pub question this). This year, while such massively popular sports as air pistol shooting, Graeco-Roman wrestling and synchronised swimming are celebrated, this sport had the ignominy of seeing its spiritual headquarters taken over by archery, a particularly dull sport to watch. A series between the current two top nations in the world was moved around to accommodate the bows and arrows. I mean, of course, cricket.

Some compensation for me came in the publication of a wonderful book on cricket, *Third Man in Havana* by Tom Rodwell. Tom Rodwell is the current Chairman of the Lord's Taverners, a leading cricket charity. I was invited to the book launch at Daunt Books in Marylebone High Street, not too far from Lord's as it was the first day of the Test against the West Indies. I met Tom when he was Chairman of another cricket charity, the London Community Cricket Association (LCCA) as it then was. I was brought in to help Tom think through the strategic direction of this charity. It was 2005, I had just started to build my portfolio career and so had time to watch cricket with Tom and discuss the charity and the role it could play.

It was also the summer the English team beat the Australians in a series believed by many to be the best ever.

The LCCA was founded in response to the Brixton riots. Its work began in the Inner London communities where it became a source of hope for otherwise hopeless and disadvantaged black youths. The skills developed in those situations were then adapted to the teaching of cricket to the blind and other disabled people. The success enjoyed in these areas brought the charity to the notice of the international community and it has worked its magic as far apart as Afghanistan and Zimbabwe. The book describes some of Tom's adventures as he visited some of these scattered places.

The vision of the charity was to use the sport of cricket to help develop individuals, groups and communities. Sport, and especially cricket, can give individuals pride and self-confidence and help them develop respect for themselves and for others. Sport gives young people a positive purpose and leads them towards healthy life choices in a world of potentially negative influences.

But why especially cricket? Cricket is a game that is played as a team game in which individuals need to perform. The individual can contribute in a wide variety of ways. Someone who may not have the hand–eye coordination to bat may have the agility and strength to bowl. Some may contribute primarily through good fielding. Cricket is a summer game that with imagination and wit can be played in all weathers, even indoors. It is a game originally played on grass that can be played on a beach, in the street etc. Cricket is a non-contact sport that can be played by people with all manner of disabilities. Cricket is a game that can be played by people of all shapes and sizes. Some of the greatest players who ever played have been small men who would have struggled in most other competitive sports.

The heritage of cricket is based on the British Empire. One of the better exports of the British was organised sport and cricket was especially successful as an implant in hot countries such as those in the Caribbean and the Indian subcontinent, where for hundreds of millions it is the number-one sport. This heritage can be exploited with the descendants of immigrants to Britain from the former colonies. Many of the stars of the game are Indians, Pakistanis, Sri Lankans and West Indians. No other sport could make such a claim.

The way the charity works is to concentrate on three "Opportunities through Cricket" programmes:

- Disability: This includes the Special Needs Schools Programme, the Youth Blind Cricket Programme, the England Blind Cricket Team, the Summer Holiday Cricket Camps and the county disability youth competition.
- Urban: This includes the Housing Estates Programme, the Urban Coaches Programme, the Inner City World Cup and Tapeball Cricket.
- Overseas: This area of work uses cricket to bring people together after a period of hostility, promote disability awareness and promote HIV/AIDS awareness.

Initial funding was from the Greater London Council but as the charity diversified, the name, the LCCA, seemed inappropriate and it became Cricket for Change. The biggest of these changes was the overseas programme. As its coaches demonstrated their ability to use cricket as a force for good in difficult places, the Foreign and Commonwealth Office became involved and asked them to go into places like Afghanistan, Cuba and Zimbabwe where their own diplomatic efforts were restricted.

It was the FCO that persuaded Tom to take his coaches to Cuba. Ever since the Bay of Pigs fiasco in 1961 and the missile crisis the following year, US policy has been to isolate Cuba from the rest of the world and particularly from the other West Indian nations. Its most popular sport is baseball. Tom surmises that the FCO plan was to re-introduce cricket and encourage Cuba to play it against its neighbours, and so in a post-Castro world undermine the US influence. I say re-introduce cricket because there was some tradition of playing cricket there. In the 1920s many West Indians had gone to Cuba for work on the sugar plantations. Many of these came from British colonies like Jamaica, only 100 miles away. Some of them built the infamous Guantanamo base for the USA. But in the Castro era cricket has declined, although it is still ranked no. 38 in the list of officially approved sports. Tom organised a game between Havana and Guantanamo and found himself having to explain terms like Third Man.

This got him thinking about Graham Greene's novel *Our Man in Havana*, a wonderfully comic story about a British vacuum cleaner salesman called Wormold who becomes involved in a surreal spy story, and the darker novella *The Third Man* about a criminal conspiracy to exploit scarce hospital drugs in post-war Vienna. Before mixing these together as the title of his book Tom went to see Greene's daughter to seek her approval. She told him that Greene hated cricket but still had fun with his distaste in *Stamboul Train* in which two dodgy characters are called Hobbs and Zudgliffe [sic] after England's greatest opening partnership.

Tom's book is full of wonderful anecdotes. In Jamaica Tom played in a game inside Spanish Town jail. The great West Indian fast bowler Courtney Walsh was helping with the project. The inmates are mainly drug dealers and murderers but when they saw Courtney they all wanted to play a game of cricket with him. Tom found himself fielding to the great man's bowling with a particularly notorious murderer at the crease. Off a short run Courtney bowled and the batsman lashed out. The ball came straight to Tom and stuck in his right hand. Mixed emotions went through Tom's mind as on the one hand he wanted to write "Caught Rodwell bowled Walsh" in his scorebook but on the other hand he feared what the outraged batsman might do. The convict walked towards Tom, put his bat down and shook his hand. "Good catch, man."

The International Cricket Council is surprisingly keen to use cricket to help disparate groups come together: indeed its mission statement is "To captivate and inspire people of every age, gender, background and ability while building bridges between continents, countries and communities." Often such statements are mere window dressing, but it was at the ICC's request that Tom and his team were invited to Israel to scope out the possibility of using cricket to help build such bridges. The match involving both Palestinian Arabs and Israelis was played about 100m from the crossing into the Gaza Strip. Only three months before, Hamas had fired BM-21 Grad rockets into the area, one of which landed next to the Be'er Sheva cricket pavilion, just on the boundary of the sandy ground. Tom bowled an over from the Gaza end and the last of the resultant sixes went right over the Israeli defences into the Gaza Strip. They were just about to ask, "Can we have our ball back, please?" when an Israeli armoured personnel carrier came careering round the corner in a cloud of dust, and screeched to a halt about where cover point had been. The platoon commander ran up to Tom's local representative, George, and started screaming at him in Hebrew. Everyone had to get on the bus and leave. Tom tentatively asked George what the officer had said. "Not much," answered George. "Just that he thought that your bowling was shit."

Soon after the 1973 Yom Kippur war, cricket became a Jewish Olympic sport for the first time. The Maccabi Jewish Olympics take place every four years with teams from all over the world taking part. It's such a shame that cricket is not featured at the 2012 London Olympics. Twenty20 would have been the perfect format with all the facilities already in place. It would have been a fantastic showcase for one of the world's greatest games and the archery could have been staged in Sherwood Forest.

Chile

Fine Wines from Chile

17th December 2011

Sebastian Faulks is one of my favourite novelists and I have always been impressed with the apparent authenticity of his work, which I assumed was based on meticulous research. Thus his great novel about the First World War, *Birdsong*, seems to bring you the very smell of the trenches; and then his magnificent study of the 19th-century treatment of mental illness, *Human Traces*, appears rooted in a detailed analysis of the fumbling of those pioneers. I was therefore very surprised when earlier this year I heard him say in a radio interview that he did little research and that most of his work came from his own knowledge and imagination. But this was confirmed for me when I read his novel *Engleby* in which the eponymous hero (or villain) described drinking a cheap bottle of Chilean red wine in a scene set in the 1960s. In fact at that time there was no Chilean wine imported into Britain, or if there was it wasn't cheap. Faulks is simply assuming that because there is now, there must have been then.

So in this, my 100th blog, I decided to write about something close to my heart, Chilean wine. I first drank Chilean wine on my first trip to Chile in 1980 and was very impressed, particularly with the reds, but even at that later date there was not much being exported. Two years later I met and married my wife while living there and brought her back to live with me in England in 1983. At that time I believe there was just one brand imported into the UK, Concha y Toro.

I don't recall who had the idea first, whether it was my wife or me. She insists it was her so I'll let her win that argument, but we decided to try and import some Chilean wine ourselves. So in the mid-1980s on a trip back to Chile my wife persuaded a well-established and locally famous brand, Viña Undurraga, to appoint her as its representative in the UK. I should say that my wife had no previous business experience except working as a secretary for big companies, although she did tell them that I was well connected with the grocery trade, which I suppose I was at the time, but as a supplier of cake mixes, not of alcoholic beverages!

Viña Undurraga

She set up a business called Fine Wines from Chile and started to import the wines, at first in small quantities as a single container filled with wine would have been a prohibitively costly investment. We started by selling them to friends and neighbours, who were all impressed with the quality. Viña Undurraga is famous for its different shape of bottle, which is more triangular, a little like Mateus Rosé, although I assure you the contents were infinitely superior. This started to be a problem as it took more space on the shelves and was frowned on by retailers we approached. Nevertheless, we enjoyed some success sampling the wines at fairs and using such contacts as we did have to widen the distribution. But it was still a very small business and probably not registering very much on the market share charts.

Then the Wine Importers Association decided to turn their attention to Chile. Australian wines had become particularly well established, Bulgarian wines were popular at the cheap end and Californian wines had also made their mark. The switched-on Commercial Attaché at the Chilean Embassy also decided to get behind Chilean wines. He saw how open the British market is to wines from other parts of the world. After all, we have virtually no domestic wines to protect. He formed a committee to consider how best to proceed and invited the two importers of record to join it, together with other major shippers, distributors and retailers. So my wife found herself sitting down with buyers from Tesco and Grants of St James's. At that point we decided that this was in danger of overwhelming us and gracefully withdrew from the market. The great thing about a wine business is that when you decide to close the business you can drink the stock.

But the committee was the start of great things for Chilean wine in this country and consumption has grown from that very low figure to fully 8 per cent of the market today, or the equivalent of one bottle in every case imported. Hardly any self-respecting wine list from pub to upmarket restaurant will not have at least two Chilean entries, one red and one white, and many will have several more.

So what is it about Chile that makes its wine so good and such good value? Chile has a history of wine making dating from the time of the Spanish Conquistadors, but the wines came into their own when noble Bordeaux vines were planted in the mid-19th century. Thanks to the natural barriers of the Andes and the Pacific, the vines were never affected by the phylloxera epidemic which devastated European vineyards in the late 19th century, and are grown ungrafted to this day. Ironically the French had to replant their vineyards with stock from Chile or California, which also escaped phylloxera, a fact seldom acknowledged by the French.

But while the grapes are descended from French aristocracy, the Chileans have particularly favourable growing conditions. Chile as everyone knows is a long, thin country that is geographically and climatically defined by the Pacific Ocean to the west and the Andes to the east. The vineyards are mainly found in the Central Valley around Santiago which is 35° south of the equator. Wines produced in Europe are all produced at latitudes much further north than 35°. This means that Chilean grapes are exposed to more sunshine but are not spoilt because of the cooling effect of the cold air from the Andes and the Humboldt Current that brings cold water from the Antarctic. Thus there is a wide temperature variation between day and night-time temperatures which has the effect of maintaining the grapes' levels of acidity. The climate is dry with an average of 38 centimetres of rain annually and little risk of springtime frost.

But the poor economic and political conditions of the 1960s and '70s affected the wine industry as much as any other. The growers could not invest in modern fermentation plants or in new barrels. Chile has no oak, from which the best barrels are made, so the producers made the best they could of their old beech wood barrels, but eventually the effect of mould or rotten wood affected the taste. Domestic taste buds may get accustomed but export is unlikely. Then in the early 1980s as the economy grew, modern methods of wine making were introduced. French, Spanish and American oenologists brought their expertise to Chile. Investments were made in modern fermentation plants, which allowed them to make the clean, fresh white wines preferred by modern drinkers, and these days the white wines will be stored in stainless steel vats. Proper oak barrels were introduced, replacing the traditional beech wood barrels, allowing good quality red wines made from Cabernet Sauvignon, Merlot and Chile's own Carmenère grapes to be aged in oak.

As Chile exported more of its wines and took part in international competitions, there was some scepticism over the authenticity of some of its varietals. Wines purporting to be Merlot and Sauvignon Blanc did not seem to have the classic taste of those two well-known grapes. On investigation, what Chileans were calling Merlot was in fact the grape Carmenère, while the Sauvignon Blanc was Sauvignon Vert, a mutated cross between Sauvignon Blanc and Semillon. Now proper Merlot and Sauvignon cuttings have been imported and Carmenère is sold in its own right.

Chilean wines now regularly beat French and other wines in competition. They are usually cheaper because their brands are still not as well known as the famous Premier Crus. One brand I particularly enjoy is Cono Sur, a nice pun as it sounds like Connoisseur but means Southern Cone, the southern part of South America. Cono Sur is produced by Alfredo Hurtado, whom I have had the pleasure to meet. Alfredo has studied wine growing in other parts of the world but now practises it to a high art in Chile. His wines are organically grown and his vineyard is carbon neutral. Of course he is sensitive to the issue of wine miles but uses lightweight glass to reduce the effects of transportation. His organic methods include using predators to catch pests, and garlic paste to deter ants. He also employs flocks of geese to hoover up some of the bugs. Spraying is a waste of time he says because you simply create a desert which before too long is re-infested with whatever pest you were trying to control. So you have to spray again.

I commend his wines but if you can't find them I'm sure you can find another nice Chilean wine to go with your turkey this Christmas. We certainly shall.

And on the subject of enjoying wine, I quote from a letter to the *Daily Telegraph* by Mr Scotford Lawrence, responding to the advice from the Royal College of Psychiatrists to restrict consumption to two small glasses per day:

> Since retiring more than ten years ago, I have taken a Master's degree, written a couple of books and translated two more, served as a trustee of a charity, lectured, and worked as a technical expert for a national museum and as an adviser to two continental museums. I garden and am active in a local sports club.
>
> But reading the advice from the Royal College of Psychiatrists, I wonder what I might have achieved had I not, as I have all my adult life, drunk several glasses of wine with dinner each night.

Environment and Sustainability Global Goals

9th January 2016

At the United Nations (UN) summit in New York in September 2015, the Sustainable Development Goals (SDGs) were launched to replace the Millennium Development Goals (MDGs), which expired at the end of 2015. The SDGs, also known as Global Goals, are a proposed set of global targets adopted by governments that will ultimately impact the way business operates. They will run from 2016 to 2030. The MDGs, which have undoubtedly resulted in general progress, fell short in some respects as they were focused on poverty alleviation in the developing world and had loose reporting requirements which meant that countries were not all responding consistently. The SDGs are different – they are globally applicable and integrate economic, social and environmental aspects.

I recently attended a workshop on the SDGs run by PwC, looking at their implications for business. I also recently attended the annual Marketing Society Conference (see my blog "Go Beyond", 12th December 2015, http://www.davidcpearson.co.uk/blog.cfm?blogID=4370) in which Amanda Mackenzie, CMO of Aviva, explained her role seconded as Executive Adviser, Project Everyone, a charity set up by Richard Curtis to promote the Global Goals to everyone in the world.

The MDGs were launched in 2000 for a fifteen-year period with high ambition in eight areas:

1. Eradicate extreme poverty and hunger

2. Achieve universal primary education
3. Promote gender equality and empower women
4. Reduce child mortality
5. Improve maternal health
6. Combat HIV/AIDS, malaria and other diseases
7. Ensure environmental sustainability
8. Global partnership for development.

They were thus focused primarily on the developing world and while there were some great achievements, business was not highly engaged. "The MDGs fell short by not integrating the economic, social and environmental aspects of sustainable development ... People were working hard – but often separately – on inter-linked problems." Areas where they fell short included a failure to consider the root causes of poverty; 1 billion people still live on less than $1.25 a day; it would take another decade for child mortality to fall by the target; the actual contribution of the MDGs is debatable as countries like China have in any case economically migrated to middle-income status; those most in need of the MDGs – the poor, most fragile countries – benefited last.

The new SDGs have been increased in number to cover seventeen areas:

1. No poverty
2. Zero hunger
3. Good health and well-being
4. Quality education
5. Gender equality
6. Clean water and sanitation
7. Affordable and clean energy
8. Decent work and economic growth
9. Industry, innovation and infrastructure
10. Reduced inequalities
11. Sustainable cities and communities

12. Responsible consumption and production
13. Climate action
14. Life below water
15. Life on land
16. Peace and justice – strong institutions
17. Partnership for the goals

Other differences include the fact that 193 countries have agreed and committed to achieve common goals with worldwide support from civil society, business, parliamentarians and other actors. The MDGs targeted developing countries, particularly the poorest, while the SDGs will apply to the entire world – rich and poor. There is a single framework in one language with a real determination to implement change and measure success in real time. The programme links development with the private sector and integrates economic, social and environmental aspects. It tackles discrimination and protects human rights. The concept of "no one left behind" has been adopted with an explicit focus on disabled and vulnerable people.

The next steps are for governments to be invited to create cohesive national sustainable development strategies supported by national financing frameworks. Each country is responsible for its own development and the role of national policies is critical. Governments will look to society, and business in particular, to help them meet the Goals. There will be a focus on the private sector, investment and innovation, economic growth and inclusion. Thus, this will represent a major change for business with a need to refocus strategy, contribute evidence and provide data. No doubt one risk is an increase in regulation but the corresponding opportunity is for businesses to be seen "to step up to the plate".

A key issue is measurement. As well as 17 areas there are 169 individual targets. A global indicator framework is to be developed by the Inter Agency and Expert Group on SDG Indicators. This is to be agreed by the UN Statistical Commission by March 2016. Governments will develop their own national indicators for monitoring progress on the goals and targets. Measurement will be nationally owned and led, thus providing the foundation for regional and global reviews.

So what does this mean for business? The member states will look to business to help them achieve the goals to which they have signed up. CEOs will want to know how their business supports or detracts from government's goals, especially if they want to be on the receiving end of "fair" regulation and a welcoming licence to operate. Such licence is not meant purely in the legal sense, but also in the sense of the court of public opinion, because consumers want business to engage.

PwC conducted a survey in 2015 to assess the level of engagement by business in the SDG process. It found that 80 per cent of businesses plan to assess its impact, but most have only some of the SDGs in mind and 20 per cent have no such intention or don't know. The survey shows, not unsurprisingly, that there is quite a difference between business and consumer attitudes to the different SDGs. When asked to rank the five SDGs that could represent a business opportunity for their company in the future, businesses prioritise decent work and economic growth; industry, innovation and infrastructure; affordable and clean energy; responsible consumption and production; and climate action. Asked to prioritise, citizens prefer zero hunger; climate action; quality education; no poverty; and clean water and sanitation. These differences could prove an area of frustration but if politicians engage with business properly, all of these areas that preoccupy citizens are also areas of business opportunity.

Citizens (or customers) have great expectations but these are not generally matched by business. Ninety per cent of citizens expect business to sign up to the SDGs and 50 per cent expect business to embed them into their strategy. But only 31 per cent of business is working on this now and only 41 per cent think they will have done it within three years. Interestingly, in this global survey UK consumers had the highest levels of expectation.

The Global Goals programme may, and indeed should, drive new business behaviour. First of all, it is impossible to see how anyone can object to the direction of these goals. The issue comes when the business leaders mistakenly asks themselves "But what's it got to do with us?" The answer is everything if you want your business to survive and prosper. It will not be possible for a business of any size, particularly with international reach, to ignore this process.

A Board should first understand the different national SDG priorities and hotspots. Then you should conduct a company analysis assessing your impact on the SDGs. You require a global view of your operations, supply chain and impacts with respect to each SDG area. Then you should check the results, define the company strategy and messaging, set goals and define metrics.

The key is to understand your impact. Traditionally, businesses have sought to maximise value to shareholders/owners, that is profit, and overlooked value to all other stakeholders. However, other stakeholders, whether customers or suppliers, employees or the community at large, are increasingly influential, determining your licence to operate and your reputation. Hence, to ensure long-term success stakeholder value must be maximised.

In the workshop I made the point, as I have made many times before, that the 2006 Companies Act brought these obligations into law. The act is the longest piece of UK legislation ever and did not come into force until 2009. It may be that its effect is still not widely understood but among other far-reaching changes it codified directors' duties for the first time. These include an obligation to promote the success of the company, to consider the community and the environment and the interests of employees, and to be fair to shareholders. It can only be a matter of time before test cases are brought against company directors by suppliers who have been unfairly put out of business or by members of the community who argue that a company's actions are damaging the environment.

Several businesses have already made announcements in support of the SDGs. These include Anglo American, ANZ Bank (Lao), Ltd., Aviva, Bayer, Fuji Xerox Co., Ltd., GSK, LEGO Group, MasterCard, Pearson, Safaricom, Suez, Sumitomo Chemical, and several more.

PwC believe that Global Goals are a Board discussion subject and suggest the following questions for your Board to consider:

- Is your Board able to evidence how they are helping or hindering governments' achievement of their goals?
- How will your company's licence to operate be affected by a government striving to achieve the Global Goals?
- Are the Global Goals a new strategic lens to review decision making?
- What's your company's risk exposure if the Global Goals are or are not achieved?

Richard Curtis is one of the most altruistic people I have met (see my blog "Richard Curtis" 29th March 2014, http://www.davidcpearson.co.uk/blog.cfm?blogID=320). Amanda Mackenzie has been seconded to his charity Project Everyone to help bring the Global Goals programme to the awareness of as many people in the world as possible. They have made a great start and believe that already over 3 billion people have been made aware. One programme was to teach the same class in the subject to over 500 million schoolchildren in many countries in the world, including North Korea. As part of my Master's year as Master of the Worshipful Company of Marketors I plan to run a one-day conference on my theme "Marketing for Good is Good Marketing" and I am delighted to say that Amanda has agreed to address the conference. Make a note of the date: Friday 2nd October, at New College, Oxford University.

Technology and Innovation
Centre for Leadership Innovation

9th April 2011

This week I was invited to attend the launch of the Centre for Leadership Innovation (CLI) at the Palace of Westminster. The Centre is being established by the University of Bedfordshire in order to develop research and practice which addresses three core questions:

- What are the challenges facing today's leaders, at all levels, and their organisations?
- What does "leadership" involve doing to enable successful, innovative and authentic organisations?
- How can forms of leadership be developed and enabled?

I was also invited to participate in a panel discussion to kick off the Big Conversation the directors wanted to hold to shape the direction of the research programme.

On the platform with me were
- Penny De Valk, CEO, Institute of Leadership and Management
- Terry Morgan, Chairman, Crossrail, and President, Chartered Management Institute
- Dean Royles, Director, NHS Employers, and Chairman, Chartered Institute of Personnel Development

- Linda Holbeche, CLI Co-Director

The event was facilitated by Dr Nigel MacLennan, CLI Fellow and prolific author in the field of leadership coaching with fifty-seven publications to date.

Penny began by discussing the shifts in world trade and demography; the development of consumerism; and the need to use your people as a source of competitive advantage. She asserted that what made us successful in the past would not work in the future. She asked us to challenge the mythology of leadership and cautioned us against two stereotypes of leaders, the "conquering hero" who arrives on his white horse to save us or the "expert" who is the one with all the answers. In seeking innovation in leadership development, she advised us to focus on three stages of behaviour:

1. Knowing, i.e. having the knowledge of what to do and how to do it
2. Doing, i.e. getting on with it
3. Being, i.e. knowing oneself, and here the need to establish trust has never been more important.

Terry thought the key was doing what feels right. As an engineer with a manufacturing background he does not accept that the UK only has a future as a service economy and wants to see manufacturing restored to the heart of the economy. He thinks the problems of the last few years have come largely from the service side of the economy. In his previous roles heading up large engineering organisations like BAE Systems and Land Rover he never had a problem recruiting the right skills but he had to do it on a global basis. He believes that what makes great companies is great leaders but not just at the top. This is well established and he would not want to see innovation for its own sake.

Dean put up a brave case for the public sector. He bemoaned the fact that few public sector leaders other than politicians are well known to the public which meant there were few role models. He asked us to sympathise with the democratic challenge that civil servants have to lead with enthusiasm whatever their political masters hand down to them as policy, while remaining true to their personal values.

Linda was concerned about the cycle of short termism which had eroded trust. How could employees trust their leaders if they could not trust them to protect their jobs? Her chief advice to a leader was to be authentic.

In my piece I told two stories: one of Akio Morita (see my blog "Memories of Akio Morita", 11 July 2009, https://davidcpearson.co.uk/blog.cfm?blogID=42), and the other of Sebastián Piñera and the Chilean mine rescue (see my blog "The Chilean Way", 23 October 2010). The best leader I ever saw was Akio Morita, the co-founder of Sony. Morita-san used to speak of the need for positiveness in leaders – he used the Japanese word *neaka*. A negative-minded *nekura* person is not qualified for management.

DP showing the latest Sony mobile phone, the CM-R111, to Mr and Mrs Akio Morita, watched by Sony UK MD, Shin Takagi, July 1993.

I believe leadership is quite easy to understand but hard to do. Leaders need to articulate a vision, engage their colleagues in committing to that vision and above all deliver with enthusiasm and precision.

So our leaders need to be able to think through the issues and unravel the complexity. They must have courage to face the truth of a situation.

They must then have the ability to motivate, not through bags of gold but by getting their people to reach beyond their known limits. They must also have energy and a willingness to get things done.

But that might suggest that we're looking for Messiahs to lead us – Penny de Valk's "Conquering Heroes" – and that is not what I mean. That way lies danger because very often such people are actually deluded, do not face the truth and lead their people over the cliff. Leaders take their people with them through patient explanation of issues, of how as much as where.

This is often done in teams – leadership is a team sport. When I was at Sony I formed the Leadership Group consisting of the top twenty-five managers in the company. They were not all accustomed to working together or involving each other in key decisions but gradually that changed, and I believe the group is still in existence today.

Political leaders seem to have lost their way and the nation's trust, while business leaders have all been tarred with the same brush as the bankers who borrowed short to lend long. But many great businesses were founded in recession. Sony was founded in the ashes of Tokyo in 1945 but with a vision to create new kinds of products from combining the science of electronics with the engineering of mechanics. From that vision emerged the transistor radio, the Trinitron TV, the compact disc, the Walkman and many more.

Thirty years ago I was living in Chile when it went through one of the deepest recessions in modern recorded history; the deepest was in the United States after the Wall St Crash. The next deepest was in Russia after the fall of the Soviet Union. The Chilean recession of 1982–83 was the seventh on that list.

But Chile over the past twenty years has become the most dynamic economy in South America. Last year it experienced an earthquake of massive proportions, 8.8 on the Richter scale. In one night 20 per cent of GDP was wiped out. I wonder how the British nation would react to such an event. But Chile has already rebuilt most of the damaged infrastructure, roads, harbours, bridges, hospitals, schools, homes and office blocks. The nation is back on its growth trend. And then faced with a mining disaster last October it demonstrated to the world how to lead by taking control of the problem and not resting till the last miner had been rescued. President Piñera followed my three steps. He set the vision, to rescue every one of the miners; he engaged his Cabinet colleagues and many others in Chile and around the world; and he executed the plan with tenacity and courage until the last man emerged safely.

The goal of the new Centre for Leadership Innovation is to explore the nature of leadership needed for healthy, effective, high-performing and sustainable 21st-century organisations which also add to the public good (health, wealth and welfare).

The Centre will do this through research and providing thought leadership, provoking debate and challenging holy cows, influencing and inspiring opinion formers in public life as well as developing real organisational leaders by stimulating new thinking and engaging them in co-creating new practice.

It is setting out to close the knowing–doing gap and create new leadership practice more appropriate to the changing needs and aspirations of tomorrow's workforce and other stakeholders. It intends to act as a leadership laboratory, with lessons from practice inspiring new research and vice versa. Judging by the quality of the debate that was stimulated in the Palace of Westminster and the first White Papers it has published, it has made a good start.

Marketing and Business
Duchy Originals

14th September 2013

This week I had the great pleasure and privilege of attending a special garden party at Clarence House, the present home of HRH, Prince Charles, the Prince of Wales and his wife, the Duchess of Cornwall. The occasion was the 21st anniversary of the launch of Duchy Originals, a range of foods and other products that Prince Charles had sponsored in 1992. I was a member of the original (excuse pun) Marketing Advisory Group that was set up to advise the Prince and his staff on the creation of the brand, the development and launch of the first products and the establishment of a successful business.

Prince Charles had strong views about farming, the balance of payments in general and food in particular, and the ability of the farmers on his Duchy of Cornwall estates to maintain high standards of food production and achieve good prices for their output. Through his involvement in the Prince's Trust he had links to Sir Allen Sheppard, who was then Chairman of the Board of Trustees, Prince's Youth Business Trust and of the Prince's Trust Council and, in his full-time role, Chairman and Group Chief Executive of Grand Metropolitan plc, the forerunner of Diageo. The Prince came up with the idea of developing a new range of branded foodstuffs and Sir Allen asked his Commercial Director, the late Keith Holloway, to find a suitable team to advise the Prince. Keith asked me and a group of leading marketers to join him at a meeting at St James's Palace in March 1991. The group included Clive Wilson, Head of Marketing Services, PA Consulting; the late Gordon Medcalf, then Director General of the Marketing Society; John Hegarty, founder and Creative Director of BBH (now Sir John); and Sue Farr, then External Affairs Director, Thames TV and Chairman Elect of the Marketing Society.

David Landale of the Duchy of Cornwall explained the position at that time which was that they had had some success with a loaf of bread branded Highgrove after the Prince's country estate. Keith presented a paper "Duchy of Cornwall Enterprises" and in that meeting and at several subsequent meetings the group debated how best to proceed. All of us could see the potential but there were several concerns about the different objectives and how to reconcile them. Principally, we were concerned about the threat of commercial enterprises seeking to exploit a brand emanating from royalty.

For centuries the Royal Family has awarded warranties to producers of products bought by the royal household. I was myself a Warrant holder from Prince Charles on behalf of Sony. I still have the Warrant hanging in my study and it states:

> These are to certify that by command of His Royal Highness the Prince of Wales I have appointed Sony United Kingdom Limited into the place and quality of Supplier of Consumer Electronic Products to His Royal Highness; to hold the said place until this Royal Warrant shall be withdrawn or otherwise revoked. This Warrant is granted to D.C. Pearson Esquire trading under the title stated above and empowers the holder to display the Prince of Wales's badge of Three Feathers in connection with the business, but does not carry the right to make use of the Badge or His Royal Highness's Arms as a flag or trademark. The Warrant is strictly personal to the holder and will become void and must be returned to the Treasurer to His Royal Highness in any of the circumstances specified when it is granted. Given under my hand this first day of January 1995. Richard Aylard, Treasurer to His Royal Highness.

By this time I had come to know Commander Aylard quite well through working with the Duchy but I am getting ahead of my story. The point is that it was another step altogether to create a brand under the Prince's own direction.

We therefore agreed a manifesto for the brand and asked that it be presented to Prince Charles. He invited us down to Highgrove where he also explained his ideas. He was concerned about the balance of payments particularly in food and wanted to set an example in marketing in the UK. He wanted to deal with what he saw as complacency in the food business and encourage it to be more competitive. He wanted through the vehicle of the Duchy of Cornwall to encourage agricultural marketing, particularly into the European market. And he wanted to use such a business venture to establish a large fund for charitable purposes which would enable him to pursue important projects. At this point organic issues were not highlighted although the Prince was and remains passionate about them, but he also recognised the practical limitations at that time of going down that route. It would have limited product volumes enormously. He was most impressed with our manifesto which emphasised quality above all in everything. It was clear to me that he had a vision to create a virtuous circle of activities: quality products from quality ingredients that are marketed well, with the value added returned to the community. It was a pioneering form of what is now called social enterprise.

Initially a projects committee was formed under Duchy supervision and then this was replaced by a Board once a trading company was established. But throughout this period, with a clear understanding of the objectives and the methods of operation, the Marketing Advisory Board was maintained and met frequently to consider issues of branding, product development, distribution, pricing and all the elements of the marketing mix. Some of these meetings took place with the Prince at various of the royal palaces including St James's and Sandringham.

Grand Met again helped enormously in seconding a very talented marketing director, Christopher Nadin, as Projects Manager. Various potential products had been identified including dairy, lamb, bread, water and soft drinks but the oatcake biscuit was prioritised. The oatcake biscuit, as it was first called, was to be made from the finest selected organic oats and wheat grown on the Duchy Home Farm at Tetbury in Gloucestershire.

It would combine the look and feel of a traditional oatcake with the lightness and texture of a traditionally baked biscuit. It was a biscuit for adults, not children.

A great deal of time went into the question of branding, but Duchy Originals was chosen as both defining the provenance and the positioning. We were not riding on royal association but were bringing genuine innovation to the market. The independent brand identity design consultancy Lewis Moberly (LM) was retained to develop a packaging design which incorporated the shield of the Duchy of Cornwall. Mary Lewis produced this design and while still at LM, is now President of the Design Jury at the Cannes Festival. LM is still retained to this day to produce designs for Duchy Originals.

The biscuit, now named Duchy Originals Oaten Biscuits, was launched in 1992. We had advised great care in distribution and although the Highgrove bread test market had been run in Tesco we advised selective distribution with emphasis on specialist food outlets where discerning shoppers were used to paying more for premium brands. Initially this policy was followed but in later years, after our group had been disbanded, this policy was relaxed and more volume sales were sought.

We also advised to keep fixed overheads to a minimum and where possible source not only ingredients but also production from third parties. The fine Scottish firm of Walkers, not the crisp manufacturer but the maker of shortbread, was selected to produce the oatcake and I am glad to say it still does, and representatives from the family firm were present at the garden party.

However, in later years after our involvement ceased, and Chris Nadin and his successor Michael Cornish had ended their secondments and returned to previous engagements, people came in who changed some of the carefully constructed rules we had crafted. They widened the franchise beyond food to include toiletries and other products that had no remote connection with the Duchy. They widened the distribution beyond the specialists and so became prey to the insatiable demands of the major chains. And they established their own factory in Launceston, in the heart of Cornwall it is true, but breaking that principle of minimum overheads. An owner of a factory becomes concerned about filling that factory, sometimes at the expense of his own brand values.

Inevitably serious losses followed. For financial year 2008–9, Duchy Originals suffered an operating loss of £3.3 million on turnover of just £2.2 million. It became necessary to make a new arrangement and a deal was struck with Waitrose which took over ownership of the brand but pays a royalty to the Duchy to enable contributions to charity to continue to be made. That has saved the brand which is back in rude health even if it now reads "Duchy Originals from Waitrose".

This week Prince Charles revealed that when he started the business Duchy Originals in 1992, many people believed it was destined to fail. He said:

> Its birthday is being celebrated this week. I suppose the journey of this brand is a good illustration of why it is worthwhile to stick with an idea you believe in.
>
> No one wanted to know about organic food all those years ago, so it was one of the very first such enterprises of its kind and a huge challenge to develop an organic supply chain from scratch.
>
> When we launched the first product – an oaten biscuit – the headlines in tabloid newspapers said "A Shop-Soiled Royal".
>
> Now the business is worth £72m and has raised more than £11m for my Charitable Foundation – a grant-giving charity – and for my Countryside Fund, which supports Britain's hard-pressed rural communities.

Prince Charles was delayed in coming to his own garden party because he and Camilla had been to the funeral of his closest friend, Hugh van Cutsem. But soon after arriving he came over to the few of us who survived from the Marketing Advisory Group, Messrs Farr, Hegarty and me with the first Project Managers Messrs Nadin and Cornish. He shook our hands and said he was most grateful for our efforts.

And I am most grateful if in some small way I have helped. The group worked together from 1991 to 1996, when Commander Aylard wrote us all a very nice letter which stated that a reorganisation had taken place but that they hoped that they could call on our advice and counsel from time to time. In my reply I said, "I sincerely hope that the seeds that have been planted so carefully now bear fruit for his Royal Highness and his charities in the way that was originally envisioned." It looks like they have.

Board Governance
The Time I Interviewed Ruby Wax

16th January 2010

Of all the pre-Christmas "do's" I went to perhaps the most interesting was a Criticaleye reception where the guest speaker was Ruby Wax. "Oh no, not the Ruby Wax who made her name in alternative comedy and then did some wacky interviews with people like Hugh Hefner and Pamela Anderson?" I hear you saying. Yes, the very same, but also the Ruby Wax who majored in psychology at the University of California, Berkeley and now works with leading organisations from Goldman Sachs to the Home Office on developing emotional intelligence and creating trust in relationships.

Ruby Wax was born Ruby Wachs, in Illinois, USA, the daughter of Jewish parents who fled from the Nazis in Austria in 1939. Her father built up a successful sausage-manufacturing business. After University Ruby came to the UK and studied at the Royal Scottish Academy of Music and Drama. She began her acting career as a straight actress opposite Alan Rickman at the Crucible Theatre, Sheffield. Alan was later to direct most of her stage comedy shows.

In 1978 she joined the Royal Shakespeare Company and appeared with Michael Hordern in *Love's Labour's Lost*, and with Juliet Stevenson in *Measure for Measure*. Ruby made an appearance in a 1980 episode of *The Professionals*, which also featured Pierce Brosnan.

She then switched to comedy and developed a brash and loud persona conforming to the British stereotype of an American. Her physical appearance matched this image, with red hair and blood-red lipstick. In the 1980s she appeared in the British sitcom *Girls on Top*, as backstage interviewer at Amnesty International's 1987 benefit show *The Secret Policeman's Third Ball* and in *Red Dwarf*. In 1987, Wax was given her own comedy chat show *Don't Miss Wax*, on Channel 4.

She now capitalises on being one of Britain's best-known TV personalities by offering leadership facilitation to top organisations. Through her directness, intuition and humour she quickly establishes a relationship with her guests, creating a climate of mutual appreciation and rapport. She claims that this incredibly useful skill can be taught to any leader who wants to motivate, inspire and improve communication within their organisation.

Ruby Wax draws on her twenty-five years of interviewing experience to facilitate leaders from organisations as diverse as Skype, Deutsche Bank and the Welsh Assembly.

Her workshops include clips of interviews with Madonna and Imelda Marcos, etc. Ruby deconstructs these clips, demonstrating moment by moment how she gets under the skin of these individuals, relating to them on a human level, breaking down the facade.

Workshops also include practical exercises to help leaders viscerally feel the difference between talking "at" someone rather than "with" someone. Participants learn to be more aware of how other employees, clients and partners perceive them and therefore how to present a more human face, utilising humour, curiosity, empathy, intuition and honesty.

She particularly emphasises developing emotional intelligence – developing skills in self-awareness, self-management, social awareness, genuine listening and social management – "working the room". As you might expect she also encourages using humour in leadership but also how to best work under stress while keeping the organisation positive and creative. She shows how to create trust in relationships and break down the barriers between employees and leader.

Examples of her work have included:

- Coaching members of a defence organisation to develop insight into their individual behaviours when working as a team and therefore be able to adjust that behaviour through awareness and self-regulation.

- Facilitating members of the government to communicate more effectively with the public and their employees by teaching them to talk "with them" rather than "at them".
- Coaching managing directors and CEOs to change their organisations to a culture of openness and creativity rather than fear, and how this change must come from the emotional intelligence of the leaders.
- Interviewing CEOs of several global Internet companies and international banks in the presence of their employees to make them more "user friendly", exposing their more human side, showing they could be trusted and that they were genuinely passionate about the organisation.

Ruby Wax has experienced episodes of depression for most of her life, but it wasn't until she finally checked into a clinic that she realised how widespread mental problems are: "It's so common, it could be anyone. The trouble is, nobody wants to talk about it. And that makes everything worse."

Ruby has written about depression and used the topic for her one-woman shows as a way of getting the subject out in the open. "We need to take the stigma out of mental illness. People shouldn't be ashamed of it." Ruby manages her depression through therapy and medication and is optimistic about the future: "It used to be the 'C' word – cancer – that people wouldn't discuss. Now it's the 'M' word. I hope pretty soon it'll be okay for everyone to talk openly about their mental health without fear of being treated differently."

After her speech I had the opportunity to talk with her. Far from being brash she is quite vulnerable and clearly sincere in her desire to encourage empathy. Humour is so often a defence mechanism but I am delighted that she has found a practical use for her talents and I am sure the leaders and organisations who work with her will benefit from developing their own emotional intelligence.

Leadership and Management
The Importance of Failure

"I have not failed. I've just found 10,000 ways that won't work."

Thomas Edison

12th January 2013

In this my 150th blog I want to turn to the importance of failure. Most of us have known failure but there is a perfectly understandable human desire to cover it up and only talk about our successes. When we write a CV or give an interview we will emphasise all our good points and seek to hide our not so good ones. But only Superman has super powers and even he was vulnerable to Kryptonite!

I am very sceptical of the person who is not willing to admit to the occasional failure, not because I don't believe them but because I believe that you learn more from failure. I have had to close down brands, factories, even companies, and while those are not my happiest memories I learnt much more from those experiences than from whatever success I have enjoyed.

I began this blog with a quote from Thomas Edison, who was taking about his eventually successful development of the electric light bulb. He experimented with 10,000 methods that did not work before he used a filament of tungsten that did. Similarly when Head & Shoulders was developed by Procter & Gamble to treat dandruff, a condition experienced by two-thirds of people some of the time and a third all of the time, it experimented with 20,000 compounds before it discovered the one that was effective, zinc pyrithione. Some years ago I had the pleasure of having dinner with Sir James Dyson who told me the story of his development of the "bag-less" cyclonic vacuum cleaner. Financed only by his wife's earnings as an art teacher, he spent five years and went through hundreds of prototypes before breaking into the market and taking it by storm. The rest is history but his success is based on Edison's many ways that wouldn't work.

Such experimentation is the norm in the pharmaceutical industry, for example, and is one reason why their resulting products are expensive. Even after they have identified an apparently effective cure they must go through highly regulated trials to see what side effects there may be.

Linked to this is the need to make sure that credit is shared. One of the finest bosses I ever worked for was John Coady, who was President for Global Development when I was at Mars. It was John who asked me to go to Chile and start a marketing company there. He used to say: "If only we did not worry who gets the credit how much more progress we could make." Success has many fathers, as they say, while most run away from failure. But this is odd because we learn so much more from failure. Bill Gates, surely one of the most successful businessmen the world has ever known, is reputed to have deliberately set out to recruit some Vice Presidents who had known their share of failure in their careers because most of his senior team had come up with the company only knowing the extraordinary success of Microsoft. Gates wanted someone around him who would be there if the wheels started to come off and say, I recognise this problem, I've faced it before and this is what we should do.

One of the finest managers I ever knew was Akio Morita, the co-founder of Sony. He wrote a short pamphlet with his thoughts on management which is much more valuable in its insights than many of the long books on the subject. He also spoke of trust but in an interesting way:

> Trust your people. This is a most important rule. Too often, top managers are overly concerned about whether or not they themselves are trusted. But if you want to be trusted, you have

to trust your people first. If you trust them they will trust you in return.

Trusting your subordinates means being magnanimous enough not to give overly detailed instructions. Relations with subordinates may easily become soured if you are overly eager to exert leadership and give exhaustive instructions.

On the other hand, I am always saying, "Don't trust anybody!" at the company. While it may sound as if I am contradicting myself, my point is that it is very important to follow up and check whenever you give instructions or ask other people to do something for you. You have to get your subordinates in the habit of always reporting back to you. See to it that the "Plan–Do–Check" cycle is carefully followed.

This ability to hold two apparently contradictory notions in one's head at the same time and resolve them is one of the principal lessons I learnt from the Japanese. By contrast, the emphasis in much of corporate America on the bottom line at the expense of everything else can lead to poor management.

We can see from these two contrasting styles, the visionary leadership of Akio Morita versus the deadline, bottom line-driven autocratic management style, the importance of leadership. Yesterday's leadership skills will not work in today's fast-moving and evolving world. Only creative leaders who are visionary and empathetic will succeed. I offer the following suggestions as to what you can do to succeed as a creative leader:

1. Instead of commanding, coach your team and organisation towards success.
2. Don't manage people, empower them. The know-how, experience and solutions are often out there; it's a matter of helping people discover them.
3. Cultivate respect by giving it, instead of demanding it.
4. Know how to manage both success and failure.
5. Show graciousness in your management rather than greediness. Be humble about your successes and whenever possible, give someone else the opportunity to shine.

Johann Wolfgang von Goethe summed it up when he wrote "Treat people as if they were what they ought to be and you help them to become what they are capable of being." The Red Arrows are a famous squadron of performance pilots. Anyone who has ever seen their display cannot fail to have been impressed by their breath-taking, dare-devil aerobatics. I met some of them once and they told me that after every single performance, without fail, they have a debrief in which they each contribute a verdict on that performance. Starting with the senior officer, they will admit to the slightest error and discuss ways in which it can be avoided in future. Such a discipline is no doubt essential in such a dangerous pursuit. But it is still a valuable practice in business. In such situations the individual is encouraged to admit his failings so that the team can benefit. However, in business the reverse behaviour is more common. People are quick to find fault in others and seek to take the credit for themselves.

In the branded companies with which I have been associated I have often found flocks of people keen to associate themselves with the launch of a successful brand – I've no doubt done it myself – while few admit to being involved with brands that had to be discontinued – a wonderful euphemism for "killed off". When I was Chairman of PastMarsters, the association in the UK of former associates of the Mars Corporation, I gave a speech to this effect at the annual dinner. I said something to the effect that there were hundreds of people who would seek to take the credit for being behind the success of power brands like the Mars bar or Pedigree Chum but few who would confess to being involved with Spangles or Cupboard Love. I was astonished and delighted when my old friend Gary Luddington stuck his hand in the air and owned up to Spangles!

A lot of failure derives from picking the wrong people in the first place. It is therefore very important to have good skills and processes in recruitment. I was trained to interview both at Procter & Gamble and then again at Mars. In Pedigree Petfoods, a group of sales managers were sent on a course in some personnel management techniques of which interviewing was one. Our instructor for the day played the role of a candidate for a position as one of our sales representatives. He outlined his fictitious CV on the blackboard and then gave us all a chance to ask him questions. By the time it got round to me all the relevant questions seemed to have been asked, so I asked my old standby that I had experienced in my own first job interview for Procter & Gamble: "What do you do for fun?" Our instructor in a rather offhand and exasperated way said that he liked to go grass-track racing, daring me to deduce anything from that. Then he announced that we had all failed because none of us had spotted the two-year gap in his CV and so failed to check what occurred at the time. His fictitious persona had gone to Borstal!

The famous politician Enoch Powell said "all political careers end in failure". In a way he was just expressing a version of the Peter Principle, that is, everyone rises to his own level of incompetence.

In their humorous book *The Peter Principle*, Laurence J. Peter and Raymond Hull formulated the thesis that employees tend to be given more authority until they cannot work competently. The principle holds that in a hierarchy, members are promoted as long as they work competently. Eventually they are promoted to a position at which they are no longer competent. And there they remain, being unable to earn further promotions. Peter's Corollary states that "in time every post tends to be occupied by an employee who is incompetent to carry out its duties" and adds that "work is accomplished by those employees who have not yet reached their level of incompetence". From this we can see the concept of "Managing upward", where a subordinate finds ways to subtly manipulate their bosses to prevent them from interfering with the subordinate's productive activity or to at least limit the damage done by their bosses' incompetence.

So there are two kinds of failure. The first is necessary as it is part of the scientific process, that of experimentation. No scientist is afraid of the failure of his experiment because he has learnt something. By extension, we should not be afraid of failure in business if we learn from it, both collectively as a learning organisation and individually as one who tries to improve his performance. The second is avoidable and entirely undesirable. A definition of madness is continually doing what does not work.

I have seen many examples of inappropriate promotion of individuals. I observed the "Friday evening salesman Monday morning sales manager" syndrome by which excellent salesmen were promoted to become inadequate sales managers. It was not that they did not have the potential. But the two jobs are quite different and they were not trained or prepared to do the second job.

People and Networking

Desmond Tutu

Archbishop Desmond Tutu, DP, Leslie Wilson. Master Marketor 2020, Mansion House, 2013. Photo credit Peter Holland.

14th December 2013

As the world looks at South Africa to honour the remarkable life of Nelson Mandela there is another extraordinary South African whose contribution to world peace has recently been honoured. Last month, on the 25th November, I was among those present at Mansion House when a special meeting of the Court of Common Council of the City of London was convened for the grant of the Honorary Freedom to the Most Reverend Desmond Tutu, Archbishop Emeritus of Cape Town, South Africa, in recognition of his exceptional contribution to peace and social justice in South Africa and throughout the world. As a young girl back in the 1960s, the Master of my Livery company, Miss Sally Muggeridge, came to know a curate in her North London parish. That was Desmond Tutu. He became her mentor and she is now a Trustee of the Desmond Tutu Foundation. Knowing that Desmond was due to come to London on an increasingly rare visit, she suggested to the Court of Aldermen that it would be opportune to recognise his considerable contribution to world peace with the Honorary Freedom of the City of London.

The Freedom of the City of London is not an honour and can be purchased. To become a Liveryman in a Livery company it is necessary to do this and so I have the Freedom of the City of London. But an Honorary Freedom is an honour and is only rarely conferred. I was among those privileged to be invited to witness the ceremony at Mansion House. The court proceeded to confer the Freedom upon Archbishop Desmond Tutu with all due ceremony.

The Chamberlain delivered an Address to the Archbishop as follows:-

> Archbishop Tutu, My Lord Mayor, Aldermen, Sheriffs, Chief Commoner, Ladies and Gentlemen. Today we confer the greatest gift the ancient and august City of London Corporation can give, the Honorary Freedom. It is one we award sparingly, because it is reserved for those who have made an exceptional contribution, rendered outstanding service and provided exceptional leadership and inspiration. On some occasions it is conferred upon leaders of nations, and few who were there will forget the dignity, grace and warmth displayed by President Mandela, when he received the Honorary Freedom during his visit in 1996. On other occasions it is conferred upon royalty, such as members of our own Royal Family, whether that is the late Queen Mother or Her Majesty the Queen herself.
>
> Today we honour a man who is great, not in the trappings of state or the riches of success. But he is great in heart, great in

spirit, and great in the generosity he has shown throughout his remarkable life: to the afflicted and oppressed of his own nation and throughout the world, and to those who oppressed him, and so many of his fellow countrymen and women. It is a model of leadership driven by the message of the Gospels he holds so dear, that to lead is to be last of all and to be the servant of all. In every day of his life, Archbishop Desmond Tutu has sought reconciliation, forgiveness and truth and turned away from rancour and violence. That is the case in South Africa, but his example also played no small part in contributing to the peace process in Northern Ireland, and ending a time of trouble that caused such damage to the City of London itself. He has lived a towering life, full of grace, mercy and truth. It is a life lived as a fiery pillar of social justice. It has inspired and lit up the lives of millions.

This City depends on capital and how it is allocated to support business, the finance that is vital in creating jobs, growth and prosperity here in London, across the United Kingdom and across the world. Archbishop Desmond Tutu deploys a different kind of capital, a spiritual capital, driven by his unwavering faith, a faith rooted in the belief that we are all, men and women, from whatever background, from whatever country, of whatever ethnicity, made to share common bonds, a common life, a common culture; to share in a community. It is a faith rooted in the Anglican Church into which he was ordained, but also in the spirit of *Ubuntu*, as he has described it, "the human spirit saying I am, because you are" of the bonds we all share and the responsibilities we have one to another.

He has said that "there are no ordinary people in my theology", a tribute to his wholly admirable view that each one of us is inherently valuable, distinctive and extraordinary. It is a most excellent doctrine. But I venture to suggest on behalf of us all that he is more extraordinary than most! And his extraordinary life has brought him global recognition, including the Nobel Peace Prize, and brings him here today.

It has been our privilege that he has chosen to spend time in London throughout his life and ministry, studying at Kings College, serving as a curate in North London and within the Diocese of Southwark, and engaging and speaking within the City of London itself, on peace, reconciliation and building cohesive communities; in unveiling the statue by Michael Visocchi at Aldgate; and, most recently, in receiving the Templeton Prize at the medieval Guildhall earlier this year.

Today the City of London honours Archbishop Desmond Tutu, but we who are gathered here represent hundreds of thousands of our fellow citizens who love and admire him and who cherish the contribution he has made as a beacon of all that is good and true. In expressing a hope that he might retire from an active role in public life in 2010 he commented that "too much of my time has been spent at airports and in hotels". Many of us in this most international, most diverse of cities know that weariness all too well. Thus we are all the more grateful that he should be with us today. Archbishop Desmond Tutu, it is my honour to ask you to sign our Roll of Fame and record for posterity the honour you do us today.

On behalf of the Lord Mayor, Commonalty and Citizens of this City in Common Council Assembled, I ask you to accept this resolution. They trust you will regard it as evidence of their recognition of your exceptional contribution to peace and social justice in South Africa and throughout the world.

I now have the privilege and honour as Chamberlain of this great and ancient City to offer you the right hand of fellowship and greet you as a Citizen of London.

The Most Reverend Desmond Tutu, Archbishop Emeritus of Cape Town, Republic of South Africa, replied as follows:

My Lord Mayor, I should like to express my huge appreciation and gratitude for the kind words to me, my wife and my family spoken by the Chamberlain on behalf of the City and Corporation of London. We are most honoured by the generous and warm hospitality of the City of London for the second time this year as has already been mentioned. Indeed, it was only in May this year that I was privileged to be in the City of London, at Guildhall, to receive the Templeton Prize. It is always a pleasure for Leah and me to be in London. For that is where we first came as a family in 1962 as I had been appointed as curator of St Alban's Church in Golders Green. There we were warmly welcomed into the Christian arms of many wonderful people including a very young Sarah Muggeridge, now Master of the Worshipful Company of Marketors in the City of London and a founder Trustee of the Tutu Foundation UK. It is Sarah who brought me here today and it is wonderful to be among so many of our friends that I have seen in the audience.

Like many of my fellow South Africans, I had been brought up in a tradition of love for Great Britain and its democratic institutions. But at the time of coming to London in the 1960s my wife and I were not free people in our own country. We relished the freedom and respect that London offered me and my family. I have often recounted how we particularly liked asking for directions from your wonderful British bobbies, even when we knew where we were going. What a pleasure to be addressed politely as sir and my wife as madam.

In London I studied for my Bachelor's degree in theology and gained my Master's at Kings College. I visited my alma mater again last week and was delighted to see that splendid institution thriving under the continuing stewardships of its Principal Sir Rick Trainor and its Dean, The Rev. Professor Richard Burridge. It's also good for the ego to see my face large and prominent in one of the windows of the building at Aldwych where there is a students' bar in the college called Tutu's.

Prior to my return to South Africa we moved from North London to a ministry in leafy Surrey at St Mary's Church, Bletchingley and we made many more friends there, some of whom are with us today.

My peace and reconciliation work has been mentioned. The Tutu Foundation UK was launched six years ago as a continuation of this. The Foundation's mission is to transform lives and communities here in the UK by building peace, respect, understanding and connections between people of different ethnic, religious and cultural backgrounds. The South African concept of *Ubuntu*, also mentioned, shows how we can be fully human, only when we value and appreciate one another, recognising that what we have in common is far greater than the differences between us.

Individuals in communities are best placed to identify the issues of tension and conflict within them and find their own practical solutions. To this end, the Tutu Foundation provides a safe space for community members to engage constructively with each other and encourages collective action to build bridges across the divides. I'm glad to pay a warm tribute to its trustees and staff, present and past.

What an honour to be granted Honorary Freedom of this great City. Much of my life, like that of my dear friend Nelson Mandela, has been in pursuit of freedom in South Africa and elsewhere. I note that one of the traditional associations with the Freedom of the City of London is that of the privilege of driving sheep over London Bridge. In a sense I have perhaps been acting with others such as Trevor Huddleston and many others, all my life as a shepherd with a difficult flock, needing to be driven in the right direction.

My Lord Mayor, may I once again thank you for the honour you and the City of London have bestowed on me before I return this afternoon with my family to Cape Town. I leave as a citizen of this principal commercial global capital with happy memories of this occasion and a deep sense of gratitude. Thank you all.

These were the formal speeches that were recorded in the minutes of the meeting but Desmond went on to deliver some further impromptu remarks that were even more moving. This was the week that the General Synod was again considering the thorny issue of women bishops. Desmond spoke with both passion and humour on this issue, encouraging all of us to recognise the role that women should play in a civilised society. I count myself as privileged to have been there and to have the chance to meet this great man. It was he who was honouring us.

The Worshipful Company of Marketors
The Year in Perspective

DP as Master Marketor with Simon Leschallas, Master Vintner, Vintners' Hall, May 2016.

Sunday 22nd January 2017

This is my last blog as Master of the Worshipful Company of Marketors. On Tuesday 24th January 2017 my last act as Master will be the very pleasant one of installing my successor, Sue Garland Worthington OBE, in Clothworkers' Hall. I shall then take my place as the Immediate Past Master.

It has been an immense privilege, a fascinating experience and a great joy to be Master. I genuinely regard it as one of the most important opportunities in my life. I have also had the huge pride in sharing it with my Lady, Carmen, sometimes at my side and sometimes representing the Company in her own right. She too has thoroughly enjoyed the year and has made many new friends in the process.

As I come towards the end of my year as Master it seems appropriate to reflect on some of the things that have happened in the year. First, a few numbers. One of the Masters I have got to know well this year is Simon Leschallas, Master Vintner. Simon is in the drinks trade and he was Master Distiller in 2009–10, just seven years ago, but in that time he reckons the workload of a Master has doubled.

This is partly because every Lord Mayor seems to want to add an initiative that will continue, not just occurring in his year. And it's partly because the Livery movement is growing strongly and all the companies are putting on more events. By the time I hand over to the Master Elect I will have attended 254 engagements in the year. I call an engagement any meeting that promotes Company business, any Company event and any external invitation where I am representing the Company as Master. Of the latter there have been 107, of which 70 largely involved food and drink.

One piece of advice I got from several Past Masters was to accept every invitation. I have not followed that as it was impossible. There were too many diary conflicts. I have actually declined fifty-seven invitations so it could have been over three hundred engagements. I am pleased to say that my Lady has also represented the Company in her own right on several occasions. You may or may not be interested in the statistic of how much weight I have put on eating and drinking for the Marketors. Well, I'm pleased to say none at all.

Though I am not a churchgoer I've attended twenty services including four funerals and memorial services. I've arranged for forty-three speakers to speak to us and made forty-six speeches myself. I've written and published forty-eight blogs to date with a total of 55,000 words. Professor Malcolm McDonald thinks I should publish them as a book and maybe I will.

The most important lesson I have learnt is the high quality of work achieved by all of the Livery companies without exception. During one's year, as the dates of installation vary widely, it is possible that one could meet 218 other Masters, 2 from each company. I have not met them all, but I've met a great many and developed strong personal friendships with quite a few which I know will endure.

The principal characteristic of a Master's responsibility is that of stewardship, i.e. you must endeavour to hand the Company over to your successor in at least as good shape as you found it. It's for others to judge but I believe I will have achieved that. Membership is stable and a great many are active in one way or another. Finances are healthy with record levels of reserves. We have had a lively programme of events with excellent attendance and several events fully subscribed. There have been several revivals and/or innovations such as debates, Outreach days, a pub quiz, a wine-tasting dinner, a very successful conference, a career change workshop, and, of course the Company's first trip to South America!

I believe we have made good progress against all our Aims.

Aim One: Actively supporting the Mayoralty and the City of London. Our efforts have been widely recognised and some individuals have strongly contributed to this, such as Past Masters Venetia Howes' service on the City Values Forum and Andrew Marsden's election in June to the Livery Committee and this month as Chairman of the Financial Services Group of Livery Companies. Court Assistant and Junior Warden-Elect Andrew Cross has helped the Corporation with design.

Aim Two: Promoting marketing education and the benefits of the profession of marketing to those in the City, the Livery and beyond. The formation of the Education Committee this year has been an important step forward in furthering this Aim. Our pro bono PR Agency Whiteoaks has also opened up several new channels of communication, both traditional and digital, for us to spread the word of our thought leadership.

Aim Three: Giving back both financially and in-kind, and making a contribution to the development of marketing. Our Trust now manages funds of over £1,000,000 and has donated over £250,000 over the past five years, this year introducing the new Oxford Advanced Management Programme for Liveryman Karl Weaver. I called for an increase in the number of volunteers for Outreach and that has indeed happened. My theme Marketing for Good is Good Marketing has been well treated at our Great Events and our conference with widespread coverage.

Aim Four: Bringing in and retaining members, fostering fellowship and planning and arranging succession. We have strengthened our culture of care with wonderful support from the Almoners. We have introduced the new status of Companion for widows and widowers of former members and already several have accepted this.

In summary we have made good progress with considerable innovation but without rocking the boat. I am especially proud of the conference and weekend in Oxford, the career change workshop, the new category of Companions and of course the unforgettable trip to Chile. And looking forward, the Company is in very good hands.

In Memoriam: Lord Montagu of Beaulieu

19th September 2015

I have published well over twenty *In Memoriam* blogs covering a range of figures, from internationally famous people that I never met but who made a big impression on me to people that I knew well or in some cases very well. For inclusion in this book I could have chosen a number of people but I chose one who was a national figure of some importance but whom I also met in his home with my wife and then 8-year-old daughter.

Lord Montagu of Beaulieu, who has died aged 88, was the founder of a world famous motor museum, and spent eight years as Chairman of English Heritage. But in my opinion he was first and foremost a brilliant marketing man. He was jailed in 1954 for homosexuality but the case was so sensational that on emerging from the court with his two fellow convicts they were cheered by the crowd, while two RAF servicemen who'd turned Queen's Evidence were roundly booed. Stuck in jail for seven months, Montagu turned his mind to how to run the family estate in Hampshire he had inherited just three years before. He studied a raft of books on estate management and concluded that he must turn the estate into a profitable enterprise. He effectively invented the stately-home business.

He was born Edward John Barrington Douglas-Scott-Montagu in 1926, a huge relief to his father who had five daughters, was now sixty-one and despaired of ever producing an heir. He was just two years old when he inherited the title, and so the family seat, Palace House in

Beaulieu, Hampshire, was looked after by his mother, Alice, and trustees until Edward was twenty-five. He was evacuated to Canada during the war and returned to England aged 15. He went to Eton, served in the Grenadier Guards in Palestine and went up to my alma mater, New College, Oxford, where he mixed with artistic and bohemian circles while also becoming a member of the Bullingdon Club. His rooms were wrecked by a bunch of drunken hearties and he was sent down as a result.

He joined PR firm Voice and Vision, rising from office boy to director in just four years. His greatest success was the launch of the *Eagle* comic in 1950, for which he hired a fleet of Daimlers mounted with enormous model eagles to tour the country. His inheritance brought an income of just £1,500, nowhere near enough to maintain the estate. He threw his home open to the public but needed some additional feature to differentiate his middle-sized pile from some of the grander houses. His solution was the car museum and that is why I came to meet him some four decades later in 1993.

The museum was originally based on a single model – a 1903 De Dion Bouton – that had been owned by his father, a major campaigner for the car. The collection grew to 250 models, ensuring that Beaulieu became one of the most popular and financially successful tourist attractions in Britain. By the mid-1960s, Beaulieu was attracting over half a million visitors a year. Lord Montagu became known as the leader of the movement to celebrate and conserve vintage and classic cars, while his advice was widely sought by stately-home owners around the country.

I remember visiting the museum as a small boy on holiday in 1960 and did not return until the time when I was Managing Director of Sony UK Consumer Products Company. When I took over in 1988 the business was recovering from the Betamax debacle and my predecessor had paid little attention to a new source of business, in-car entertainment, also known as Mobile Electronics (ME). He had assigned just one sales manager and an assistant and relied on a conventional me-too strategy competing with well-established Japanese brands in that space, Kenwood, Pioneer, Panasonic and others.

The business group in Tokyo was headed up by a charismatic engineer, Hideo Nakamura, who had been one of the engineers who developed the compact disc format. I used to go and see Mr Nakamura and tell him how well we were doing in the UK in every other product group. He would get angry and say he didn't care. Why were we doing so badly in ME? Finally, I persuaded him to send one of his best engineers, Joe Usui, to head up marketing in the UK. Joe's English was a little weak so we assigned to him a decent British Marketing Manager, John Anderson (later to take charge of all audio marketing in Europe), and the two of them developed a new strategy, to supply Sony in-car products to car dealers as an option upgrade. This was extremely successful and sales grew fast. Mr Nakamura came to visit us. We took him to Aston Martin to see the cars made with Sony products fitted as standard. We took him to the National Motor Museum at Beaulieu, where Lord Montagu allowed him to drive a vintage Jaguar, and we took him to the Waterside Inn at Bray where he ordered a trout by humming the opening bars of Schubert's Quintet. He became an Anglophile on that visit and went back to Japan and changed his BMW for a Jaguar. Our annual Mobile Electronics sales went from £1 million to £53 million and we became the leading market for Sony ME outside Japan.

In 1993 Sony launched a new audio format, Mini-Disc. The ME group developed an in-car model and Mr Nakamura asked me to deliver the first one in the UK to Lord Montagu as a thank you. I drove down there with my wife and then 8-year-old daughter at Lord Montagu's invitation for lunch. His son and heir, Ralph, also joined us. The lunch was delicious, with trout caught fresh from the Beaulieu River.

DP presenting first in-car Mini Disc player in UK to Lord Montague of Beaulieu at the National Motor Museum, February 1993, accompanied by Coca and daughter Michelle.

In conversation we discovered that we had both been to New College and compared notes. But I think his experience of Oxford, with the Bullingdon Club and so on, was very different from mine as I had survived largely on coffee and cheese rolls.

We have some splendid photographs to help recall the occasion, and some of Lord Montagu and me in one of his cars, showing off the Mini-Disc player, were used in publicity releases.

He was one of the few hereditary peers to remain in the House of Lords and headed numerous heritage organisations and charities, particularly English Heritage. When Margaret Thatcher abolished the Greater London Council in 1986, she transferred the management of the capital's historic buildings to English Heritage, "because Edward Montagu will know what to do with them".

Education

A Mathematics Problem

"Do not worry about your difficulties in Mathematics.
I can assure you mine are still greater."
Albert Einstein

29th November 2014

I went back to school this week. At the St Albans School for Girls where I have been a Governor for 12 years they held a Governors' Day. This was led off with a breakfast organised with the Hertfordshire Chamber of Commerce to demonstrate the attractiveness of STEM (Science, Technology, Engineering and Maths) careers for girls. The Hertfordshire Chamber of Commerce acknowledges the importance of raising and broadening girls' career aspirations and the importance of encouraging more young women towards a career in a STEM area. As such the Herts. Chamber has been working with schools on a pilot programme to link schools and STEM businesses together. Six young ladies each gave a short talk on their own STEM career and were all accomplished, confident and inspiring.

Kate Bellingham is an engineer and television presenter most widely known for her role presenting the popular BBC science show *Tomorrow's World* from 1990 to 1994. Sophia Mountford is an asset engineer at Affinity Water; she has attained a Master's in Civil and Architectural Engineering and went on to complete a graduate scheme at Affinity Water. She specialises in water and sewage systems. Denise Austin is the Director of Pearldrop Video Production. Her role includes meeting with clients, organising shoots and spreading the word about what a video can do for your organisation. She read Maths at University and says she uses it every day. Roisin Speight is an engineer at Airbus Defence and Space. As a young girl she dreamt of going into space. Now she is helping to design rockets and satellites that do go into space. Danielle Calvert is a third-year engineering apprentice at MBDA Missile Systems. She works in the manufacturing department and very soon will be going on to the live build centre. Only nineteen, she has won the Best Apprentice in the East of England Award. Cally Gentle is a higher mechanical engineering apprentice, also at MBDA Missile Systems. She is working towards her second year of the Mechanical Higher National Certificate.

This was an excellent session and the school is setting the pace locally in encouraging girls to take STEM subjects and seek STEM careers. But we also need to encourage more boys to take STEM subjects and seek STEM careers. This is not just a gender issue, which has always been there; it is a national crisis, particularly in our shortage of qualified engineers. I was struck by this recent letter to a national newspaper:

> The reason for the shortage of engineers and scientists in Britain is that Applied Maths was replaced by Pure Maths at secondary level in the 1970s.
>
> Applied Maths uses maths to solve problems. It is essential to teaching and learning engineering and the sciences. Pure Maths is the study of mathematical conundrums, with no practical application.
>
> This short-sighted policy destroyed Britain's engineering and scientific expertise, and has produced two generations of mathematically illiterate adults. The skill shortages have had to be made up by migrant workers.
>
> Applied Maths should be reintroduced at secondary level and Pure Maths offered only at A-level and above.
>
> Peter Wedderburn-Ogilvy, Froxfield, Hampshire,
> letter to the *Daily Telegraph*
> 18th November 2014

I decided to look into this. First let's look at the difference between Applied and Pure Mathematics. One way to look at it is that Pure Maths is maths done for its own sake, while Applied Maths is maths with a practical use. But it's not quite that simple, because even the most abstract maths can have unexpected applications. For example, the branch of mathematics known as "number theory" was once considered one of the most useless, but now plays a vital part in computer encryption systems. If you've ever bought something online, you can thank number theorists for letting you do it safely.

Another way is to think how maths relates to other subjects. Applied Maths seeks to model, predict and explain things in the real world: for example, one area of Applied Mathematics is fluid mechanics, which analyses how fluids are affected by forces. Other examples of Applied Maths might be statistics or probability theory. Pure Maths, by contrast, is separate from the physical world. It solves problems, finds facts and answers questions that don't depend on the world around us, but on the rules of mathematics itself. Unfortunately, there is no perfect way to decide what Pure Maths is and what Applied Maths is. Even mathematicians can't agree on it.

Back at the school I asked the Head Teacher if what was said in the letter was correct. She could not confirm the dates but said it had been largely the case since she started teaching in the 1980s. I later had a meeting with the Head of Mathematics on another subject and then picked his brain on this issue. He confirmed it and blamed the National Curriculum. He went further and said there was not time to take students through an explanation of mathematical principles so that they could apply them in different situations. I asked him if there was any chance of Ed Miliband achieving his promise of training an extra 400,000 engineers by 2020. None whatsoever, he said, while the National Curriculum is as it is. In any case, engineering graduates in the year 2020 are already in Key Stages 3 and 4 where there is very little Applied Maths prescribed in the syllabus.

Of course, some schools go outside the National Curriculum and make sure their students can compete for those universities where, to take Mathematics, Physics and other subjects like Economics, a high standard of both Pure and Applied Mathematics is required. But the majority do not cover this to a sufficient standard as far as I can see and so the nation will continue to be short of the skills it needs to compete in a global market.

Still in education, I also attended a meeting of the University of Bedfordshire Court where I am a member. Our new Chancellor, John Bercow, the Speaker of the House of Commons, gave a polished performance in his first Court meeting, as did Bill Gammell, former Minister of Higher Education, who has been Vice Chancellor for two years. Local MP Kelvin Hopkins, by complete coincidence, asked a question about Mathematics. It's not a subject the University teaches but his point was that the University does train teachers and there is a national shortage of Maths teachers. Our standards of mathematics and numeracy now rank below the international average. The question stimulated a lively debate in which I joined, given the above. Engineers in the room confirmed the problem and one local businessman said in twenty-five years he had been unable to recruit one British Engineering graduate. A quarter of his workforce was Polish, all graduates but all willing to roll up their sleeves and get their hands dirty. Others present thought it was a cultural problem as modern parents all wanted their sons and daughters to become doctors and lawyers rather than engineers, who they see as messing about with hammers and spanners.

John Bercow said as Speaker he could decide on Adjournment debates and he hoped an MP might bring this subject forward as one for the House of Commons to debate. If that happens it was, as Bill Gammell told me afterwards, "a good morning's work".

Philanthropy
CANCERactive

15th April 2017

In the 1970s when I was a young brand manager at Pedigree Petfoods, a division of Mars Inc., one of my advertising agencies, Ted Bates, appointed a new Account Director to work on my business. Chris Woollams had previously worked for Grey and Ogilvy & Mather in London and New York. I found his attitude refreshing as he really wanted to understand my whole business, not just sell me an advertising campaign. We became good friends and he even accompanied me on overseas trips to visit sister companies. On one of these his wife came with us with their baby daughter, Catherine. We worked out that we were contemporaries at Oxford and almost certainly played football against each other. I was at New College and Chris was at St Peter's Hall where he read Biochemistry. I still have records of my football career and played against St Peter's Hall four times. In 1968–69 we lost 0-4. At the end of that season I was a member of our five-a-side team that reached the semi-finals and then drew 2-2 with St Peter's Hall in a third-place play-off and so shared third place. In 1969–70 I scored in a 4-3 win but then in 1970-71 we lost 1-3. As we were contemporaries Chris probably played in all four games.

He went on to become the youngest chairman of a London agency at Ted Bates but left after Saatchi bought it and then founded his own agency, WMGO, which was listed on the Stock Exchange in 1994. Chris cashed out and "retired" in 1995. After a sabbatical he formed The Woollams Outsourcing company (TWO) but was starting to think about a life outside business. He spent more and more time researching his twin passions, fitness and health. Then in the spring of 2000 his whole world changed when Catherine, now 22, was diagnosed with a brain tumour and "given" six months to live. St Thomas' Hospital had never had anyone live longer than 18 months. Chris got to work using his research abilities coupled with his knowledge of biochemistry and nutrition. Catherine lived for three and a half years.

Two doctors suggested Chris wrote down what he had found out. This led to the best-selling book: *Everything You Need to Know to Help You Beat Cancer*. This in turn led to requests to speak in the UK, then the USA, and Australia. Chris has now spoken all over the world, addressing audiences of 3,000 people in Moscow to 28,000 in Japan; always on the subject of how to best empower yourself to beat cancer. As he says, "There's so much information out there – I just want to pass it on."

He founded the charity CANCERactive which he had planned with Catherine in her final months. It is now the largest charity of its kind dedicated to providing information to people to help them prevent cancer or beat it once diagnosed. This has now become a full-time career. But he refuses to be paid for it. All monies from speeches and books are passed straight on to the charity CANCERactive to fund a quarterly magazine (*Icon*) and a 2,000-page website.

A few years ago I was present at Lord's cricket ground when England cricket legend Geoffrey Boycott opened his speech with "I am only here tonight because of Chris Woollams. Chris Woollams saved my life." Chris is only interested in the facts and believes that many of the professionals deal in myths, not facts. He develops personal prescriptions (PP) for his patients. About two years ago, CANCERactive received an email from one of Chris' first ever PPs. That would be about 14 years ago! He'd had "terminal" prostate cancer, the oncologists had nothing left to offer and he'd been sent home to write his will. "Chris was the first person to actually tell me I could beat it," he wrote. He followed the plan and for the last six years he said he has forgotten he ever had prostate cancer.

CANCERactive has "terminal" patients in the USA, Australia, Korea, India, Portugal, Spain and Canada that certainly aren't terminal now. What's the secret? Chris says there's no secret. "You just cover off all the bases, do the important things and help someone build a really healthy body. That tends to take care of the cancer. It's really not rocket science but of course there are those who want you to believe it is. But be clear. I don't deal in false hopes. I deal in research. Solid quality research is really important to me."

Chris finds serious quantitative research that might have led to the banning of the use of a particular chemical in, say, cosmetics in, say, Japan when the same stuff is still freely sold in the US or the UK. He'll find serious quantitative research that proves that a particular drug is not only ineffective but positively harmful. He'll find evidence that cancer is likely to have been caused by stress or poor nutrition or other lifestyle choices and so it is by addressing these causes that it can be cured rather than by horrendously invasive, damaging and painful chemotherapy or radiotherapy.

While people like Geoffrey Boycott like to call Chris the "cancer guru", he himself makes no such claims. He is not a doctor, nor does he claim to be one. He has no special healing abilities. Nor does he offer to "cure" people. But he was an Oxford University Biochemist who after his first degree was offered the chance to go on and do a DPhil (PhD in Oxford). He chose to go into the communications industry instead but he had the foundation knowledge. When his daughter was diagnosed with cancer he started researching potential treatments all over the world, and he found so many that could help a young girl in serious trouble. These were treatments with quality research behind them that could make a difference, but for all sorts of reasons were not being passed on to patients.

There are major research studies that show that people who actively manage their stress survive much longer. National Cancer Institute scientists produced a report on the benefit of a good diet and bioactive natural compounds. The American Cancer Society produced a meta-study report in 2012 stating that "since 2006 there had been an 'explosion' in research into complementary therapies and 'overwhelming' evidence that they could increase survival and even prevent a cancer returning."

This report exposes one of the greatest myths of modern medicine; namely the mindless mantra that "we are beating cancer due to earlier diagnosis and better drugs". According to Chris it is simply not true and there is no rigorous research supporting this claim.

In researching this blog I found a biography of Chris online[1] where I am quoted: "Says David Pearson, formally Chief Exec of Sony in the UK, 'Chris is a great bloke. He has turned personal adversity into the opportunity to benefit thousands of people.'" I stand by that.

---

1. http://www.chriswoollamshealthwatch.com. To contact Chris about a PP, email him on chrismeanshealth@gmail.com . I was Managing Director as it was a subsidiary but never mind.

Language and Culture
World Heritage List

26th August 2017

What do Stonehenge, the Galapagos Islands, the Pyramids of Giza, the Great Barrier Reef of Australia, the Palace of Versailles and the Temple of Angkor have in common? They are all among the 1073 Common Assets of Mankind that UNESCO has inscribed on its World Heritage List.

This list has grown over time so as to reflect the diversity of the planet's cultural, natural and intangible treasures. It comprises 832 cultural assets, 206 natural assets and 35 mixed assets in 167 Member States. Since March 2012, 190 Member States have ratified the World Heritage Convention.

I referred to this briefly in my blog "I've got a little list" in December 2012, when I said:

> I have set one personal ambition that I will never fully achieve but will have lots of fun trying. That is to see all the World Heritage sites as decided by UNESCO. The World Heritage List includes 962 properties forming part of the cultural and natural heritage which the World Heritage Committee considers as having outstanding universal value. These include 745 cultural, 188 natural and 29 mixed properties in 157 States Parties. As of September 2012, 190 States Parties have ratified the World Heritage Convention. When I set this ambition a few years ago there were about 750 World Heritage sites so the committee is making it very difficult for me to achieve this particular ambition

as they ratify sites faster than I can see them. But it should keep my wife and me busy for a few years yet.

In less than five years UNESCO has awarded World Heritage status to 111 more assets, so as I said, my ambition is unachievable as they award this status faster than we can get round them.

Last week my wife and I joined a river cruise on the River Rhone through Provence and Burgundy. We saw no less than five World Heritage sites. We started with Arles with its Roman and Romanesque Monuments, the Great Amphitheatre, the Necropolis and the Forum. From there we also visited the magnificent Pont du Gard, a Roman aqueduct seen by the Romans themselves as their greatest architectural achievement. We then visited the Historic Centre of Avignon: the Papal Palace with its outstanding architecture and fine collection of frescoes and tapestries; the Episcopal Ensemble and "le Pont D'Avignon". Here we learnt that the words of the song are wrong. The dancing did not take place "*sur le Pont*" (on the bridge) but "*sous le Pont*" (under the bridge) as the bridge is too small for dancing in the round and so they danced under it on the island. We then visited The Climats: terroirs of Burgundy, passing through villages with magical names like Montrachet and Meursault before touring Beaune, which claims to be the wine capital of the world, where of course we had a fine-wine tasting in one of the caves in the centre of this wonderful city. Finally we visited the Historic City of Lyons with its Roman theatre, and both a magnificent cathedral and a spectacular Basilique. Five World Heritage sites in one week can't be bad.

It was on the 16th November 1945 that representatives of thirty-seven countries gathered in London to sign the Constitutive Act of the United Nations Educational, Cultural and Scientific Organisation (UNESCO). This took effect on the 4th November 1946 after ratification by twenty signatory countries. In 1954 The Hague Convention established early protection of cultural assets. In 1960 the proposed rescue of the Abu Simbel temples in Egypt stimulated the involvement of UNESCO in the protection of World Heritage. In 1965 the World Heritage Foundation was created. This was followed up in 1972 by the Convention for the Protection of World Heritage cultural and natural international treaty. The Convention came into force on the 17th December 1975. To date it has

Pond du Gard

been ratified by 193 states parties, including 189 UN member states plus the Cook Islands, the Holy See, Niue, and the Palestinian territories. Only four UN member states have not ratified the Convention: Liechtenstein, Nauru, Somalia and Tuvalu.

In 1973 the list of World Heritage Assets was created. In 1992 the notion of cultural landscape was introduced. In 2003 these arrangements were further strengthened with the Convention for the Safeguarding of Intangible Cultural World Heritage in a further international treaty.

In the UK we are used to a long tradition of protecting and maintaining our cultural assets with the establishment of charities like The National Trust and public bodies like English Heritage. Other countries have come much later to this concept but it does appear that real progress is being made. We learnt for example at the Pont du Gard that it used to be overrun with campers and stalls, while now there is a superb visitor centre and a museum and access is strictly controlled. That does not mean that people cannot enjoy themselves as there were numerous young people canoeing on and swimming in the river below the bridge.

According to the sites ranked by country, Italy is the home to the greatest number of World Heritage sites with 53 sites, followed by China (46), France (43), Germany (42), India (36), Mexico (34), and United

Kingdom and British Overseas Territories (31). Other prominent countries are the Russian Federation (28), the USA (24) and Iran (21).

My ambition will be further frustrated by the concept of Tentative Lists. States Parties are encouraged to submit their Tentative Lists, properties which they consider to be cultural and/or natural heritage of outstanding universal value and therefore suitable for inscription on the World Heritage List. Out of 193 States Parties to the Convention, 182 have submitted a Tentative List. These Lists comprise a further 1,669 sites, a potential increase of 155 per cent!

Just two sites have been delisted: The Arabian Oryx Sanctuary in Oman was delisted in 2007, and in 2009 the Dresden Elbe valley in Germany was delisted. However, several sites are deemed to be in danger. The List of World Heritage in Danger is designed to inform the international community of conditions which threaten the very characteristics for which a property was inscribed on the World Heritage List, and to encourage corrective action.

Armed conflict and war, earthquakes and other natural disasters, pollution, poaching, uncontrolled urbanisation and unchecked tourist development pose major threats to World Heritage sites. Dangers can be "ascertained", referring to specific and proven imminent threats, or "potential", when a property is faced with threats which could have negative effects on its World Heritage values.

The World Heritage Committee lists fifty-four properties in danger and not surprisingly they are mainly located in troubled states including Afghanistan, Central African Republic, Côte d'Ivoire, Democratic Republic of the Congo, Egypt, Iraq, Jerusalem (site proposed by Jordan), Libya, Mali, Palestine, Syria (no less than six sites), Venezuela and Yemen. But rich nations should not be complacent as in the UK, Liverpool – Maritime Mercantile City, only listed in 2012, is seen as in danger, as is the Everglades National Park in the USA, only listed in 2010.

Nevertheless, my wife and I will continue to work our way up and down the list, and for my part I think this initiative is one of the better outcomes of the whole UN project.

Pedantry

It Doesn't Add Up

25th July 2009

In my last blog I referred to the significant number of students entering University to study Science today who cannot perform simple mathematical tasks. But this lack of numeracy is much more widespread than that and is a real threat to our economy at large and to business. According to the *Independent* on Monday 20th July 2009:

> The economic pressure on the Treasury was further underlined when the National Audit Office (NAO) delivered an embarrassing rebuke to the department over its handling of the bailout of Britain's High Street banks. It refused to sign off part of the Treasury's annual accounts, because a £24bn insurance scheme granted to Lloyds and Royal Bank of Scotland to cover toxic loans was not approved by Parliament. The refusal marked the first time in a decade that the Treasury's accounts were qualified.

The credit crunch as a whole is largely down to mistakes in assessing risk and an inability to understand the complexity of the structured instruments that had been invented to re-package debt. An early example of this had been Long-Term Capital Management, which was a US hedge fund which used trading strategies such as fixed income arbitrage combined with high leverage. It failed spectacularly in the late 1990s leading to a massive bailout by other major banks and investment houses, which was supervised by the Federal Reserve. Ironically its Board of Directors included Myron Scholes and Robert C Merton, who shared the Nobel Prize for Economics in 1997. Initially enormously successful with annualised returns of over 40 per cent (after fees) in its first years, in 1998 it lost $4.6 billion in less than four months following the Russian financial crisis and became a prominent example of the risk potential in the hedge fund industry.

I have been both amused and disappointed to observe simple errors of mathematics reported in our national press. Back in March 1998, a Labour MP, one Derek Wyatt, came up with a new millennium target: a computer in every home paid for by National Lottery funds. He claimed that this "would cost no more than the Millennium Dome – and would be a better use of the cash". He said, "A typical home PC costs about £1,000, meaning it would take roughly £240m to provide every home with one. The funding for the Dome totals £700m."

I was moved to write to the *Independent* who had reported this. "If funding was to be found to provide £1,000 PCs for 23.5 million homes, it would cost £23.5bn, not £240m, which clearly represents only a £10 unit cost for the PCs. Let's hope the Millennium Dome does not make the same scale error in its forecasts."

But it did and they still do.

Just recently *The Week*, an otherwise admirable summary of the week's newspapers, reported on the problem of the loudness of the grunting of female tennis players at Wimbledon. They said that Michelle Larcher de Brito's grunting was measured at 109 decibels, "only 11 decibels quieter than the noise of a plane taking off". To make this worse, their caption for a photo of Ms Larcher de Brito read: "almost as loud as a plane taking off". Perhaps it's complicated but the decibel scale is logarithmic which is useful mathematically because it means a huge range of outcomes can be measured on quite a tight scale, just as the Richter scale covers massive variation in earth tremors.

Three decibels represents approximately a doubling of energy i.e. noise level, so moving from 109 to 112 would be a doubling of noise levels; then to 115 a doubling again; then to 118 a doubling again; then to 121 a doubling again. Thus the noise level of a plane taking off is about sixteen times as loud as her grunts. Even if their reporters were ignorant of all this, did not even a moment of reflection suggest that it was unlikely?

Sport

Slow Play

2nd July 2011

This is a great time of year for sports lovers with Wimbledon, golf and international cricket particularly to the fore. I enjoy all of these, whether live or more often watching on TV, though it can be perverse when the sun is shining and one stays in the dark watching people enjoying themselves in the sun.

What aggravates this is the toxin of slow play that has crept into all of these games and others over the years.

The other night Rafael Nadal, defending champion and No 1 seed at Wimbledon, was warned for his slow play by a Spanish-speaking umpire. His response was a tirade of abuse in Spanish. Of course, the umpire did not follow up his warning even though Nadal studiously avoided any attempt to speed up his play. Players are allowed 25 seconds between points but Nadal routinely exceeded this by several seconds. Matches that used to be completed in two hours often exceed four today even though the tie-break was introduced in 1971 to curtail the first four sets to no more than thirteen games.

Golf too suffers from excessively slow play. Players can be warned and even fined but seldom are. Eighteen-hole rounds used to take about two to three hours and now usually take five or more. Players prowl around the green several times before hitting a putt. As golf is played sequentially with the players following each other round the course, a single slow player can hold everyone up. In friendly club play, he is expected to wave you through if he is more than one hole behind the match in front. But this rarely happens in championship golf even when balls are lost.

Cricket to the uninitiated may always have seemed slow but actually is a very athletic sport at which only the fittest can succeed. Players have to concentrate for long periods and bowlers run several miles a day in the course of delivering their balls. In test matches twenty overs per hour would be the norm in the post-war era and, with six hours of play scheduled, up to 120 overs would be bowled. If three runs per over were scored the crowd had a reasonable expectation of seeing about 360 runs in the day and would also be certain of leaving at close of play at 6.30 p.m. Step by step that over rate has declined. Today, teams are expected to bowl fifteen overs per hour, a decline in number of about a quarter, but they still fall short of that. In the recent series between England and Sri Lanka only about fourteen overs per hour were being bowled. Captains were changing their field placings almost every ball. Drinks intervals were being called constantly. So play would be extended into the evening and often then called off for bad light.

In cricket, captains can be fined a portion of their match fee for slow play but this rarely happens and never seems to make a difference. The authorities have discussed bringing in penalties within the game such as a deduction in runs scored for slow play but that would almost certainly bring about even more perverse results as then batting captains would encourage their batsmen to find ways to delay the game, asking for sight screens to be moved; feigning injury; calling for replacement gloves and a myriad of other delaying tactics.

What is going on?

One reason is the increased so-called professionalism in all the sports. Wimbledon was closed to professionals until 1969. Prior to that if you wanted to earn a living from the game you tended to make your reputation in the major tournaments at Wimbledon, Paris, Melbourne and New York and then retire from the amateur game and take your chances on the professional tour in exhibition matches. This is one of the reasons why it is impossible to compare great players of today with those of yesteryear because today's players can earn millions playing each other throughout their careers while previously the best players were not actually playing in the best tournaments. Many point to Rod Laver, who won Wimbledon in 1961 and 1962, turned professional and only returned to Wimbledon at the beginning of the so-called Open era to win it again. The implication is that he would have won all the intervening tournaments. But it is by no means certain that he would have won in 1961 if his fellow Australians Lew Hoad and Ken Rosewall had not already themselves turned professional. Hoad and Rosewall beat Laver in most of his early professional matches with them.

With such huge rewards in tennis all kinds of gamesmanship has slipped into a game that before was largely played for honour and fun. Today's players are mollycoddled, have vast entourages, massive egos and apparently need to wipe themselves dry after hitting one poor return of service. It all goes to defraud the public of entertainment. The structure of competition at Wimbledon has not changed. The same number of players compete over the same number of days knocking each other out in the same number of rounds until one is declared champion. But it has been necessary to bring play forward to 1 p.m. and then 12 noon on outside courts to fit in all the matches.

Another culprit, perhaps even guiltier, is TV advertising. In the UK, Wimbledon is shown by the BBC which does not take advertising breaks but significant revenue comes in from US network television which does. They need all the breaks to show the advertising to pay the fees and make a profit. Thus the players are obliged to sit down for two minutes between every two games to enable American broadcasters to take a commercial break.

Golf has many such breaks naturally and does not need to take them artificially but the same trends have occurred, which make me think that some leverage has been brought to bear on players to slow their play and allow more advertising interruptions.

Cricket now is barely shown on BBC television. Most of it is on the commercial satellite channel which abuses its market position by charging high subscriptions and still interrupting entertainment for advertising breaks.

Association Football (soccer) has never really taken off in America because there is only one major interruption in the game, that of the half-time break. That used to be 10 minutes and is now 15, the one concession that football has made to TV, but it has formally resisted American pressure to introduce other ad breaks. Research shows that in football, 38 per cent of the time is lost in breaks of play but most of these are brief stoppages when the ball is out of play or a foul has been committed and a free kick given to restart. Goal celebrations, substitutions and feigned injuries compound these but the referee can add on time to compensate for these.

Television has also slowed some of these games in another way; that of the review of the umpire's decisions. This is justified on the basis that if we can check, we should. This seems to me like saying if we can bomb Iraq, we should. Competitive sport depends on the concept that the referee's decision is final and there is no appeal. But television has destroyed that with a consequent deterioration of behaviour. In cricket, television technology is not only used to show what has happened but what would have happened! Another rule in sport should be that there is no difference between the game at the top professional level and the ordinary amateur level. The laws and the equipment should be the same. Because we cannot have instant replays in park games which can take several minutes in cricket, we should not have them in any matches. Again football has been right to hold out against this. A few questionable goal-line decisions have been used to argue for introducing TV reviews into the game but once the thin end of this wedge is allowed in there will be a clamour to review every possible offside, handball and all the other incidents that television delights in showing from every angle.

But the Daddy of them all is American football which has allowed itself to become totally distorted by television. The rules of the game call for an hour's play split into four 15-minute quarters. There is little continuity or spontaneity in American football. The game is broken up into "plays". Each play only lasts a few seconds and is then followed by a huddle in which players are informed by their coach what to do next. Even when the players are set to resume, the quarterback can wait thirty seconds before starting again. When the game is analysed you will find that much less than 30 minutes of action has taken place. But this will take the best part of four hours to show on TV. If you attend a game in person you will see the players just waiting around for the signal to go from the TV stations to the officials that they can start again. I stopped watching it years ago. And if tennis, golf and yes, even cricket go that way I'll stop watching them too.

(P.S. I wrote this in 2009 and everything has got worse. A recent Wimbledon Men's Singles final took almost five hours. In test matches we are lucky if we get twelve overs an hour. Now captains can be suspended but even with this threat nothing changes. And in football the dreaded Video Assistant Referee has been introduced with calamitous results. In theory, the onfield decision of the referee should only be changed if there is "a clear and obvious error". But in practice goals have been disallowed when one attacking player has his big toe in front of the defender. This is only revealed by repeated slow-motion replays. But, therefore, the error was not clear and obvious. It affects enjoyment of the game as the thrill of the goal is taken away after up to three minutes of analysis by another referee who is not even in the same stadium!)

Future

The Threats and Opportunities of the Internet

2nd March 2012

It is a well-established but little-understood fact that when new technologies emerge the impact on society is usually exaggerated in the short term and underestimated in the long term. The Internet is such a technology. From 1995 to 2000, dotcom venture capitalists enjoyed skyrocketing gains in their share prices, leading them to act faster and with less caution than normal. Losses were almost seen as good as they indicated attempts to build share. As has happened on numerous occasions before, unsophisticated investors piled in to buy highly speculative dotcom shares. On 10th March 2000, the NASDAQ index closed at a peak of 5048.62, more than double its value at the start of 1999. By October 2002 $5 trillion was lost in the market value of such dotcom companies. Many went to the wall having burnt through their venture capital without ever making a profit.

For me all this was clear. I could see that the Internet was a force for change but that it would not happen as quickly as all these dotcom entrepreneurs and their investors hoped. If I had known how to make money out of such a view I could have made a fortune but that would have required deeper pockets and perhaps greater nerves than I possessed. Nevertheless, I did go on the record to this effect. I wrote an opinion piece in the Marketing Society's excellent journal *Market Leader*, which was published in autumn 1999. That article is shown in full on the following pages.

The Threats and Opportunities of the Internet

Just as the US space programme led to the invention of Velcro and the development of mobile phones, so the US defence programme led to the creation of the Internet. The Pentagon wanted an alternative communications system in the event of direct strikes on the telephone network. The academic community then realised the potential of this storage and communication. Its potential for commercial application has been recognised only recently.

However, much of this is vastly exaggerated. In the Tulipmania that surrounds the Internet, we are asked to believe that a business with little trading history, negligible sales and start-up losses of millions is worth over £2 billion. Excited prophets forecast that e-tailing will take over next week, even though less than 0.1 per cent of total retail sales are so far made through the Net.

These forecasts have been with us for some time. I remember in my time at Sony that colleagues would quote a consultancy who forecast that by 1999, X or Y billion pounds' worth of goods would be sold over the Net. That certainly has not happened.

Let us suppose that these forecasts will come true, if somewhat later than originally stated. Suppose that even 20 per cent of retail sales were converted to the Internet. This would trigger huge threats to the established order.

Brand owners would find their brands under enormous threat, as their carefully nurtured selective distribution policies would lie in tatters. Obviously, if they choose to sell direct, they put at risk relationships with their customers, retailers and end users, the consumers, as they have no experience of selling direct.

The retailers would be in huge danger, because their main assets are their property. If 20 per cent of their turnover moved from the High Street to cyberspace, not only would their profits slump, but the value of their property would plummet. The barriers to entry for new e-tailers would be very low if this property base were no longer required.

But our pensions are heavily invested in these property portfolios. A major social consequence would be a serious dislocation in pension funds. This would be exacerbated if they reacted by diving into the South Sea bubble of Internet stocks.

Media owners would lose massive revenue as brand owners and retailers sought to establish alternative Internet strategies.

Surely the government would have to act. Much of the Internet revenue would flow abroad, leading to loss of profits and avoidance of VAT, and so the total tax take would fall.

In my view, there are many countervailing pressures that will prevent, or certainly slow down, the development of so-called e-tailing. Some businesses lend themselves to it, but only if the direct model is already established. Dell computers is quoted as transacting 30 per cent of its sales over the Net, but the Dell model has always been direct-to-home and, in this sense, the Net is only a logical extension of an already successful model. A leading credit card issuer now sees 1 per cent of turnover going through the Net, but this accounts for 47 per cent of fraud and returns. This company, at least, could not afford to allow much more growth. Instead there are two much more probable and positive economic developments of the Internet.

First, it should be harnessed as a way to implement dramatic improvements in the management of the supply chain. The real development of e-commerce in the US is in this arena, not direct selling. Business-to-business transactions are being transformed. In the supply chain time is money, and in my industry it takes us an hour to make a shoe but a year to bring it to market.

Second, the Internet provides a powerful tool to manage direct relationships with consumers. Too much relationship marketing in the past has simply been aimed at selling more. Great brands in the future really will have a relationship with their consumers in which the consumers are informed, enlightened, entertained and even consulted by their favourite brands. The consumers will take charge, and the brands that understand and embrace this will enjoy the fruits of the relationship.

It may be that these are seen by some as the musings of a dinosaur. To that I would say that the dinosaurs roamed and ruled the world for millions of years, while so far mankind has only managed a few thousand.

So how did I do? Well, though I say it myself I think I got most of it right. E-commerce has become established but my main point that e-tailing would not take off as quickly as forecast was correct. Online retailing was invented as far back as 1979. By the time of my article twenty years later it had only penetrated to 0.1 per cent. In 2000 came the dotcom crash and Amazon did not make a profit until 2003. In the US, online retailing is now estimated to have reached 9 per cent of total sales. That is exceeded in the UK which is interestingly the most developed in the world at just over 10 per cent. This is well below my hypothetical figure of 20 per cent but already we can see some of the dangers I foresaw.

- Brand owners. Some have chosen to sell direct while continuing to sell through traditional channels, causing confusion and other problems in relationships. Consumers are using retailers to learn about different products, particularly big ticket items, and then going home to buy online. That is clearly not sustainable and in the long run we all lose because if the retailer goes under there will be nowhere to see the products before buying them.
- Retailers. I said they would be in danger and they are. Many have already gone to the wall, particularly those who only sell items like books and DVDs that are so well sold by Amazon and the like. But interestingly, not all the business transfers online. When Woolworth closed, much of its DVD sales was lost and so the studios have learnt belatedly that they need to nurture the remaining outlets like HMV because not all customers will buy online.
- Property. The High Street is struggling and 1 in 7 shops on the High Street is empty. Many of the rest are charity shops; the country's second-largest bookseller is Oxfam. Yesterday's footfall is today's Google search. David Cameron has appointed Mary Portas to come up with strategies to save the High Street and the Mayor

of the relatively prosperous town where I live, himself a lifelong shopkeeper, is working hard locally to maintain the High Street as a thriving asset for the town. But all this is too little too late and I fear that the tipping point is not far away. If a retailer loses 20 per cent of his turnover he will probably not survive. You don't have to lose 50 per cent to be in trouble. Some will be able to compete by making themselves attractive destinations. And of course the High Street has no God-given right to survive. A quarter of the 40 million visitors last year to the newly refurbished St Pancras International railway station didn't go there to catch a train but to enjoy the shops and restaurants.

- Media owners have lost revenue. Google in the UK attracts more advertising revenue than ITV.
- Tax take. This is clearly under pressure. Google runs its European operation from Ireland and pays very little UK tax. Many of the bookmakers have gone offshore to Gibraltar from where they run online betting "shops". And HMRC have only recently closed a loophole whereby online retailers distributed DVDs etc. through Jersey to avoid VAT.

And I think my forecasts of more positive trends were pretty accurate. First, e-commerce in the B2B sector has developed very strongly and with positive benefits to the economy. There has been considerable innovation in such technologies as electronic funds transfer, supply chain management, Internet marketing, online transaction processing, electronic data interchange, inventory management systems and automated data collection systems.

Second, brands are building direct relationships with consumers through social media sites like Facebook.

In 1999, I was working for Pentland as Managing Director of its International Brands including Speedo, Ellesse, Berghaus and Lacoste Footwear. Shortly after I wrote the article I went to a trade fair in Munich where I met some of the directors of Boo.com. They wanted to distribute our brands through their online site. I questioned them about their business model, how they would manage returns etc. It was clear that they had little understanding of the fashion apparel market even though that was their chosen category. I declined to supply them. One of their directors said that maybe they would buy us instead. The following May Boo.com was placed into receivership and liquidated. The company had spent more than £80 million of venture capital in just 18 months.

By contrast, Amazon does understand its business and much of it is to do with traditional retailing. Last year I had dinner with Brian McBride after he had retired as CEO of Amazon in the UK. Brian has worked in the technology and telecom sector for thirty years with high-level roles in Xerox, IBM, Dell and T-Mobile. Amazon starts with the customer and works backwards. It concentrates on selection, pricing and availability. One of its advantages over a High Street retailer is its ability to service the long tail. While 35 per cent of CDs sold and 40 per cent of DVDs are from the top 50 that any High Street store or supermarket could sell, it makes its money on the back catalogue.

And Brian's forecasts?

- The High Street can survive but only if the retailer works out what its role is. Some will survive by combining forces with pure online retailers like eBay. Others will offer those things you can't buy online like haircuts and manicures.
- Moore's Law[2] will continue to work and you can now buy 16 GB for £12 when ½ GB cost £62K when he started out.
- Mobile will take over from the PC. In 2008 only 1 in 6 were connected to the web through their mobile. By 2014 it will crossover vs. the PC.

(P.S. I think Brian got his forecasts right and I got most of mine right, but I could not believe that the Competition Authorities and the politicians would stand by and let this happen. The economic consequences have been dire.)

---

2   In 1965, Gordon E. Moore – co-founder of Intel (NASDAQ: INTC) – postulated that the number of transistors that can be packed into a given unit of space will double about every two years. Today, however, the doubling of installed transistors on silicon chips occurs at a pace faster than every two years. Moore himself did not claim this was a Law.

The Perils of the Internet

9th May 2015

As we wake up to the potential chaos of the collective decision we voters in the Barely United Kingdom have made in the General Election, I turn to something even more dangerous: the Internet. It may be ironic that I choose to comment on this through the medium of the Internet. There is no doubt that the Internet has brought many good things, but overall I fear that the bad outweighs the good and the really important point is that it is out of control. Here is my list of ten things to fear:

1. Global Warming

Everyone knows that when they drive a car or take a plane journey they are contributing to the increase in global warming caused by carbon emissions. However, few, it seems, realise that their use of the Internet has the same effect. It seems that most people buy the idea that the Internet is "virtual" and that they can store their data in a "cloud". These terms are extremely misleading. The Internet is a physical network of servers, all consuming energy and throwing off heat and carbon emissions. The exponential increase in the volume of data circulating this network is seeing a vast increase in these carbon emissions. The biggest cause of this is the growth in the use of video on the Internet. Huge numbers of people use services like YouTube, particularly on mobile devices. According to the latest edition of the Cisco Visual Networking Index, global Internet traffic is expected to increase threefold in the next five years following fourfold growth in the previous five. This year Cisco predicts that global IP traffic will hit 1.0 zettabytes per year. This is not virtual but physical and corresponds to massive emissions of greenhouse gases. A single search using Google releases 0.2 grams of CO_2 into the atmosphere, according to Google's own figures. One estimate I saw was that by 2020 the Internet would account for 20 per cent of global emissions compared with 2 per cent for air travel, but that estimate was made back in 2009 and the use of data centres has multiplied much faster since then. This is urgent but out of control.

2. The Internet of Things

In the concept of the Internet of Things, everything will be joined up. This will transform the way we live and work but we cannot know if the benefits will outweigh the dangers. Marc Goodman points out:

> For all the untold benefits of the Internet of Things, its potential downsides are colossal. Adding 50 billion new objects to the global information grid by 2020 means that each of these devices, for good or ill, will be able to potentially interact with the other 50 billion connected objects on earth. The result will be 2.5 sextillion potential networked object-to-object interactions – a network so vast and complex it can scarcely be understood or modelled. The IoT will be a global network of unintended consequences and black swan events, ones that will do things nobody ever planned. In this world it is impossible to know the consequences of connecting your home's networked blender to the same information grid as an ambulance in Tokyo, a bridge in Sydney, or a Detroit auto manufacturer's production line.

3. Monopolisation

During every minute of every day in 2014 the world's three billion Internet users sent 204 million mails, undertook four million Google searches, shared 2.46 million pieces of Facebook content, published 277,000 tweets, posted 216,000 new photos on Instagram and spent $83,000 on Amazon. Andrew Keen, in his book *The Internet is Not the Answer*, argues that the net was meant to bring "power to the people, a platform for equality. Instead it has handed extraordinary power and wealth to a handful of people, while simultaneously, for the rest of us, compounding existing inequalities – cultural, social and economic. Individually, it may work wonders for us. Collectively, it's doing no good at all." It naturally leads to monopolies. Its chief characteristic is "winner takes all". Google, which now handles 3.5 billion searches daily and controls more than 90 per cent of the market in some countries, including Britain, is valued at $363 billion – more than six times General Motors, which employs nearly four times as many people. Facebook, the world's second biggest Internet site, used by 19 per cent of people in the world, 50 per cent of whom access it nearly every day, is valued at $230bn, more than Coca-Cola, Disney and AT&T. Uber, started five years ago and employing just 1,000 people, is valued at $40bn, twice the value of Hertz and Avis combined. Airbnb, employing just 700 people, is valued at $20bn, equivalent to the Hilton Group which owns nearly 4,000 hotels and employs 150,000 people. The messaging app WhatsApp, bought by Facebook for $19bn, employs just 55. The Internet is a perfect global platform for free-market capitalism – a pure, frictionless, borderless, economy. Imagine it is 100 years ago, and the post office, the phone company, the public libraries, the printing houses, Ordnance Survey maps and the cinemas were all controlled by the same secretive and unaccountable organisation. That's Google, and "it doesn't just own the post office – it has the right to open everyone's letters".

4. The Death of the High Street

This tendency to monopolisation is particularly acute in retailing. A 2013 American survey found that while it takes, on average, a regular bricks-and-mortar store forty-seven employees to generate $10m in turnover, Amazon achieves the same with fourteen. The individual consumer loves Amazon because it's convenient to order from your home and to receive the goods in a couple of days at your home. But the economics of this don't add up. Amazon lost $500m last year. One senior retailer I know has challenged his suppliers to show him how to make money with his online offer. No one has accepted the challenge. Instead of millions of consumers driving their cars or taking a bus or, heaven forfend, walking to their local stores, we have thousands of delivery vans making deliveries of tiny quantities. It isn't just the book shops that are disappearing. Amazon wants to sell everything and everyone is suffering.

5. Economic Decline

All over the world growth in the economy is sluggish or non-existent. There are many reasons for this: the misbehaviour of the banks, poor management of public finances, ludicrous decisions by central banks, demographics, wars etc. But another key reason is the destructive forces of the Internet. When retailers like Woolworth and HMV stopped selling records, not all that business went online. Amazon is driving down prices for the benefit of its customers but that entire margin has been sucked out of the economy and all those jobs have been destroyed. According to one recent report, 7,500 retailing jobs in the UK are at risk as 200 out-of-town stores will be closed this year by the supermarkets and DIY chains. Airbnb destroys hotel jobs. Uber destroys taxi-driving jobs.

6. The Death of Creative Industries

When everyone, including me, can write a blog, why would you pay to read anything any more? Young people seem to think it's perfectly OK to download content illegally for free. When there's no exchange of cash for your article, your photograph, your film, your book, your song, how else are you going to make money if you're a creative artist? The number of photographers' jobs in the US has fallen by 43 per cent; the number of newspaper editorial jobs by 27 per cent. In Britain, a third of newspaper editorial jobs have been lost since 2001. The US singer-songwriter Ellen Shipley calculated in 2012 that one of her most popular tracks was streamed 3.1 million times on the Internet radio Pandora, for which she received the princely sum of $31.93, roughly a dollar for every 100,000 hits. Publishing houses, record labels, newspapers are run by people who care about quality content. They're being swept away and replaced by anonymous people spreading rumours, and celebrities, with millions of followers, selling their brand.

7. The Death of Innovation

In the 20th century a small number of inventors and scientists – often working in isolation with limited funding – gave the world the car, radio, atomic power, cinema, antibiotics, television, aeroplanes, computers, air-conditioning and the Internet. In the 21st century millions of scientists, entrepreneurs and engineers – all connected by the Internet – should be able to give us tremendous scientific and economic progress. So far all we've had are the relatively useless Facebook and WhatsApp. In the US, job numbers are lower; productivity is down, particularly in manufacturing and construction. The position is no better in the UK.

8. Cybercrime

Politicians like to quote crime statistics to say that crime is down. But I think it's just moved online. The same characteristics of the Internet that allow unregulated businesses to grow from nothing to destroy established regulated categories apply to crime. This comes from Interpol's own website :

> Cybercrime is a fast growing area of crime. More and more criminals are exploiting the speed, convenience and anonymity of the Internet to commit a diverse range of criminal activities that know no borders, either physical or virtual. New trends in cybercrime are emerging all the time, with costs to the global economy running to billions of dollars.
>
> In the past cybercrime was committed mainly by individuals or small groups. Today, we are seeing criminal organisations working with criminally minded technology professionals to commit cybercrime, often to fund other illegal activities. Highly complex, these cybercriminal networks bring together individuals from across the globe in real time to commit crimes on an unprecedented scale.
>
> Criminal organisations are turning increasingly to the Internet to facilitate their activities and maximise their profit in the shortest time. The crimes themselves are not necessarily new – such as theft, fraud, illegal gambling, sale of fake medicines – but they are evolving in line with the opportunities presented online and therefore becoming more widespread and damaging.

For the burglar it's a no-brainer. Why go to the trouble of breaking and entering with all the risks involved when you can achieve much more from the safety of your desktop computer? And cybercrime does not include all the crimes facilitated by the Internet, as when, for example, the terrorist downloads the recipe for making a bomb.

9. Angry People

Last weekend my wife and I visited Lincoln Castle to see one of the four surviving original copies of Magna Carta. I'll blog about Magna Carta around the 800th anniversary of its sealing in June, but while we were there we learnt that in the 18th and 19th centuries public hangings were seen as a form of popular entertainment. People would travel for miles to see the show. The hangman would cut up the rope into small pieces and go around the pubs at night to sell these as souvenirs – hence the expression – "money for old rope". But eventually decency prevailed and the hangings were held in private with just a few witnesses in attendance. Public shaming had largely died out until the arrival of the Internet but now it is rife on social media. Trolls hide behind anonymity to bombard otherwise innocent people who may have committed some minor blunder. Death threats are common. So are suicides.

10. The Internet is Rewiring your Brain

In 2010 Author Nicholas Carr wrote, "The Internet is an interruption system. It seizes our attention only to scramble it." Some might think the online world helps us to adapt to become better multi-taskers, all while we still maintain critical thinking skills. Here are four uncomfortable facts:

1. The Internet may give you an addict's brain. MRI research has shown that the brains of Internet users who have trouble controlling their craving to be constantly plugged in exhibit changes similar to those seen in people addicted to drugs and alcohol. This is particularly a problem for online gambling, which has exploded.

2. You may feel more lonely and jealous. Social media make it easier to connect with others, but recent research by German scientists suggests that constantly viewing images of others' vacation photos, personal achievements, etc. can trigger strong

feelings of envy, even sadness. Researchers have even described the phenomenon as "Facebook depression".

3. Internet use may heighten suicide risk in certain teens. Based on a review of previous research on studies of teens' Internet use, researchers at Oxford University concluded that online time is linked to an increased risk of suicide and self-harm among vulnerable adolescents.

4. Memory problems may be more likely. A 2009 Stanford University study shows that the brains of people who are constantly bombarded with several streams of electronic information may find it difficult to pay attention and switch from one job to another efficiently. The recent proposal to allow pupils to use an online browser in the examination room is a scandal.

So what's to be done? At the individual level one can take all this into account, limit one's reliance on and exposure to the Internet. I, for one, have never used Facebook or Twitter and never will. Nor will I use Uber or Airbnb. Does that make me a Luddite? Well the Luddites' concern was for humanity rather than to stand in the way of progress. And that should still be our concern today. But I'll carry on blogging.

Day One

1st January 2011

New Year's Day 2011 is the 1st January 2011 or 1-1-11 for short. So it really is Day One. The first day of a new decade is always exciting, so what does this decade presage? It is very hard to foresee what may happen in a specific twelve-month period but perhaps not so difficult to see what will happen over ten years, though I would not hazard to say in which particular year the events might happen. At first sight it might seem that the Four Horsemen of the Apocalypse are getting up a fair head of steam. Conquest, War, Famine and Death are represented in the Book of Revelations as if the world will come to an end, but the truth about the human condition is that these are all permanent features.

Over the past decade we have had the horror of 9.11 and the appalling response to that, which has led to a ten-year war in Afghanistan that shows no sign of end, the shocking crimes committed in Iraq and many other flashpoints. One can look at the Korean peninsula, the muscle flexing of Iran and China in their own different ways, the permanent issue of shoehorning two opposing tribes into the same land whether it's called Palestine or Israel. But at the annual Churchill lecture I attended recently at the Guildhall, Baron Guthrie of Craigiebank, distinguished former General and Chief of Staff, sees the Indian–Pakistani conflict as the most dangerous. Both sides have nuclear weapons. Both governments are weak. There are many traditional rivalries and some new ones over borders and resources leading to frequent border incidents, and I would have to agree with him.

Threads and Patches

But we in the so-called West cannot be complacent as governments are in trouble wherever you look in the developed world. I don't think it's an exaggeration to say that democracy is in crisis. And as Churchill said, "Democracy is the worst form of government except for all those others that have been tried."

But this is hardly a ringing endorsement. Democracy is supposed to have an ancient tradition, being first practised by the Ancient Greeks, but they would not have recognised what we call democracy. They distinguished democracy, rule by the people, from autocracy, rule by a single person, but the people were only those men who held property or, if you like, had a stake in the system. In England we are proud of our democratic tradition, dating it back to Magna Carta, but most of this document is about the restriction of the King's powers versus the great landowners, the barons. The modern concept of universal suffrage, in which everyone over a certain age – first twenty-one, now commonly eighteen – has a vote whether or not he/she has a stake in the system through property or a job, whether or not they are educated or even literate, is in historical terms still quite new. The only ones who are excluded are the Royal Family, members of the House of Lords and those in prison, and even the latter has been challenged in the courts.

The problem is that the democratic politicians give stuff away to get elected; in plain words they bribe the electorate. Over time this has built up a level of debt that is unaffordable and now the whole developed world is in this position. It has to be reformed but that can only be done by taking back what has been promised and that only leads to less confidence in the system. I therefore predict that in the next decade we will see a series of challenges to the system with which we are familiar. Meanwhile, the Chinese, who do not have this problem, can continue to make progress, developing their own version of state-controlled capitalism.

The recent flurry of leaks of official communication in the irresponsible media has put both of these situations, war and democracy, at further risk. Wikileaks is an appalling attack on responsible government. It has increased the chance of war because war is best avoided by confidential discussion between nations through experienced diplomats. The Cuban missile crisis was defused by skilled diplomacy. If the Russian ambassador to Washington and the State department had thought that their exchanges might later be leaked to the public, war might not have been averted. Equally, democracy can only survive if we can trust our politicians. That is already under pressure but now it seems to be fair game to print any old gossip and thus destroy the basis of trust between the elected and the electorate.

The banking crisis of 2007–9 will return. Why? Because none of the problems that caused it have been addressed. Worse, the incidence of moral hazard has increased as central banks have pumped liquidity into the commercial banks, which they can relend at much higher rates, making easy returns and paying themselves vast bonuses for this idiotically simple business. I have sympathy with the banks in one respect. They are being asked to strengthen their balance sheets to avoid one of the causes of the previous crisis. At the same time they are widely criticised for not lending to help restore growth. They cannot do both but irresponsible politicians who may or may not understand what they are saying attack them for this apparent duplicity. The last crisis was a failure of the banks and of their regulators. Neither has responded sensibly and so it will happen again.

So far this blog probably seems pretty negative and I have not even touched on global warming, shortages of energy, water, minerals, food and other key resources, over population and other esoteric hazards like the disturbing decline in the bee population. Suffice it to say that these trends are all negative and I think there will be several crises under each of these headings in the coming years. It will need this to happen for the public at large to wake up to the need to change behaviour and for the politicians to take the courage to take the necessary actions to start to deal with the issues. Regulation works in this area, and private industry will respond to both regulatory mandate and to consumer pressure. I see positive signs of that with some of the best companies making remarkable commitments to sustainable development and I think this debate is more in the balance; i.e. there will be problems, but also there will be solutions.

The astute businessman will respond to all these challenges by first taking the opportunity to reflect on the macro-economic situation and then how your own organisation fits into the picture. After the worst economic crisis in living memory there are some signs of recovery with the BRIC countries leading the way. A new force of emerging markets is developing well behind them. The Western developed world still looks sluggish with a crisis in government everywhere you look. In the UK recovery is under way but from a position well below the peak in 2007. All the growth needs to come from the private sector. It's done it before but at a time of much less regulation and state interference. Banks will continue to struggle to reconcile two conflicting objectives of rebuilding their balance sheets to a more secure level while increasing their lending to business to stimulate the recovery. CEOs need to ensure that their balance sheets are strong, their strategic positioning clear, their management aligned and focused, and their service to customers best in class.

(P.S. OK I broke my own rule and these last three blogs have been pretty serious about the challenges I saw us facing at the start of the current decade following the banking crisis. That that has not repeated is welcome but we have just been kicking the can down the road in the USA, EU and UK following a disastrous monetary policy, inflating debt and asset prices without dealing with fundamental questions of a lack of proper investment. Investment does not mean public spending. Some investment comes from the taxpayer but governments are lousy at managing it, so it does not pay off in the way politicians hope. Our best chance is to hope that the private sector will be allowed to create investment leading to jobs and prosperity and then we can argue how we share that out. But if you take away the incentives, then there is little motivation to take the risks.)

Part V

Philosophy

Politics

"Confound their politics,
Frustrate their knavish tricks,
God save the King."

Henry Carey, c.1693–1743

I was brought up in the Church of England, saw the light as a teenager and have been agnostic ever since. I became a firm fan of Manchester United Football Club as a small boy and have remained faithful throughout the ups and downs of their form. But my politics has seen much more variation.

My parents were no doubt conservative with a small "c" but in fact my father was a very effective supporter of the non-political independent Ratepayers Party in the Heald Green ward of the Stockport borough. Ever since 1929, and still to this day, the Ratepayers have won every local election, sending three councillors in rotation to the council. My father was invited to be one of these but rejected it because of the pressure of his work. Instead he selflessly supported his friends Bob Crook, Bill Bushell and others as councillors. The party was successful in solving many local problems and in attracting local amenities such as a theatre which housed the Heald Green Theatre Club. It was an excellent example of local politics in action without the dogma of the national parties.

As I became politically aware I became heavily influenced by some close friends at school. They tended to come from poorer backgrounds and were already active socialists. In the 1964 election I supported the Labour Party as it won a small majority in its fight to end "thirteen years of Tory misrule", as it was characterised by a highly effective TV performer in

Harold Wilson. In retrospect, this was an inevitable result after the decline of the Tories in the early 1960s with the Profumo affair, the illness of Harold Macmillan and the misguided election of Alec Douglas-Home as party leader. Wilson went to the country again in 1966. I took an active interest and attended a meeting at St Catherine's Church Hall where the candidates made their appearance. The sitting incumbent, William Shepherd, Conservative, had represented the constituency of Cheadle since 1950. According to rumour he had only spoken in the House twice. After some years he had made his maiden speech on the subject of the colour of telephones. He was clearly exercised by this topic as some years a later he rose to his feet to speak on the subject of the colour of telephone boxes. However, this is a canard. On investigation for this thread I found that Shepherd served as a senior member of the Conservative Parliamentary Committee on Trade and Industry and wrote extensively on industrial and social matters. In the 1980s, he joined the Social Democratic Party.

His Liberal Party challenger, Dr Michael Winstanley, was known as "The TV Doctor". He was charismatic and altogether more impressive. He would have got my vote. At this stage, while interested in national politics, I still carried the idea that the vote was for the man rather than the party. General Election 1966: Cheadle Party Candidate Votes: Liberal – Michael Winstanley, 32,071, 42.4 percent, +7.8 per cent; Conservative – William Shepherd, 31,416, 41.5 per cent, -5.3 per cent; Labour – Sholto Moxley, 12,244, 16.2 per cent, -2.2 per cent. **Majority** 655; 0.9 per cent; **turnout** 82.4 per cent. Liberal gain from Conservative.

Wilson won a handsome majority, which allowed him and his socialist cronies to bring in a number of left-wing measures that screwed up the economy and led to the devaluation of the pound in 1967. One of these was selective tax on employment, an extraordinary action for any party but particularly for the Labour Party. The theory was to divert employment to more productive sectors of the economy by taxing all employment and then rebating the tax to some sectors like manufacturing. However, my father was a partner in a firm providing essential services to the construction industry. So the builder received the rebate but my father paid the tax. No party that could produce such a stupid measure would ever get my vote, nor has it.

My first opportunity to cast this vote came in the 1970 election and still loyal to Winstanley, I voted for him but he lost to a respectable Tory candidate, Tom Normanton, who went on to hold the seat until 1987. General Election 1970: Cheadle Party Candidate Votes: Conservative – Tom Normanton, 39,728, 46.3 per cent, +4.8 per cent; Liberal – Michael Winstanley, 37,974, 44.2 per cent, +1.8 per cent; Labour – Roger Stott, 8,062, 9.4 per cent, -6.8 per cent. **Majority** 1,754, 2.0 per cent; **turnout** 79.9 per cent. Conservative gain from Liberal.

By the 1974 election I was working in industry and living in Mosborough on the outskirts of Sheffield. This fell within the boundaries of Sheffield Attercliffe, one of the most cast-iron Labour seats in the land. I felt my vote was irrelevant and as a protest I was one of 424 souls who voted for Tariq Ali, a Marxist of dubious reputation. General Election February 1974: Sheffield, Attercliffe Party Candidate Votes: Labour – Patrick Duffy, 34,120, 71.9 per cent; Conservative – P.M. Santhouse, 12,944, 27.3 per cent; International Marxist Group – Tariq Ali, 424, 0.9 per cent. **Majority** 21,176, 44.6 per cent; **turnout** 74.8 per cent. Labour hold. If the Monster Raving Loony party had fielded a candidate he would have got my vote.

There were two elections that year as Wilson sought a larger majority. By the second I had moved back home and was once more in the Cheadle constituency. By now I felt my vote could make a difference at a national level and for the first time voted Conservative. General Election October 1974: Cheadle Party Candidate Votes: Conservative – Tom Normanton, 25,863, 49.2 per cent, -0.5 per cent; Liberal – Christopher Green, 18,687, 35.5 per cent, -3.0 per cent; Labour – Paul Castle, 8,048, 15.3 per cent, +3.4 per cent. **Majority** 7,176, 13.7 per cent; **turnout** 52,598 80.2 per cent. Conservative hold.

In the historic election of 1979 which brought Margaret Thatcher to power I had no doubt that this was necessary for the country. On the eve of his defeat at the 1979 General Election, James Callaghan remarked: "Perhaps once every thirty years there is a sea change in politics. It does not matter what you say or what you do. There is a shift in what the public wants and what it approves of. I suspect there is such a sea change and it is for Mrs Thatcher."

I was living in Oakham, which was firmly in the Tory shires constituency of Rutland and Stamford, and voted for a solid Conservative, Kenneth Lewis. General Election May 1979, Party Candidate Votes: Conservative – Kenneth Lewis, 26,198, 56.5 per cent; Labour – Malcolm R.C. Withers, 11,383, 24.5 per cent; Liberal – P. Blaine, 8,801, 19.0 per cent. **Majority** 14,815, 31.9 per cent; **turnout** 78.1 per cent. Conservative hold.

Ironically, having lived through the worst of the socialist disasters of the 1970s, I was to leave the country in 1980 just as Mrs Thatcher was getting down to sorting out the mess. I returned in time to vote for her again in 1983. We were living in Wallingford in the newly created constituency of Wantage and helped to return Robert Jackson, who held it until handing over to Ed Vaizey in 2005. General Election June 1983: Wantage Party Candidate Votes: Conservative – Robert Jackson, 25,992, 52.9 per cent; SDP – Winifred Tumin, 15,867, 32.3 per cent; Labour – A.J.D. Popper, 7,115, 14.5 per cent; Wessex Regionalist – 183, 0.4 per cent. **Majority** 10,125, 20.6 per cent; **turnout** 76.9 per cent. Conservative win new seat.

By 1987 we had moved again to Reigate where we supported the irrepressible George Gardiner. General Election June 1987: Reigate Party Candidate Votes: Conservative – George Gardiner, 30,925, 59.3 per cent, +0.3 per cent; Social Democrat – E.A. Pamplin, 12,752, 24.4 per cent, -2.5 per cent; Labour – R.P. Spencer, 7,460, 14.3 per cent, +2.2 per cent; Green – G.F. Brand, 1,026, 2.0 per cent, 0.0 per cent. **Majority** 18,173, 34.9 per cent; **turnout** 52,163, 72.5 per cent, -0.4 per cent. Conservative hold, swing +1.4.

In 1990 the Tories ousted Mrs Thatcher and while many will have mourned that day I mourn the day she decided to stay on too long. Most political careers end in failure. Enoch Powell said it was all! But Thatcher's failure, apart from the poll tax, was to fail to bring on her successor. In business we are as much judged by our legacy as anything and that must include our management succession. No one could have believed that John Major was the right successor to Thatcher.

John Major held on to power in 1992 and I supported him with some reluctance as I could see that the Tories probably needed some time out of power to regroup. They were in a mess over Europe, at that time the true fault line in British politics. General Election April 1992: Reigate Party Candidate Votes: Conservative – Sir George Gardiner, 32,220, 57.1 per cent, -2.2 per cent; Liberal Democrats – Barry Newsome, 14,566, 25.8 per cent; Labour – Helen Young, 9,150, 16.2 per cent, +1.9 per cent; Social Democrat – M. Bilcliff, 513, 0.9 per cent. **Majority** 17,664, 31.3 per cent; **turnout** 56,449, 78.5 per cent, +6.0 per cent. Conservative hold, swing +1. Later George Gardiner defected to join Jimmy Goldsmith's Referendum Party. I was firmly anti-Europe at this time. I thought the Maastricht Treaty was a treaty too far. However, I could not bring myself to vote on a single issue in a General Election.

Major held on for his full five years. It is interesting to speculate what would have happened if Neil Kinnock had won in 1992. Surely by 1997 the country would have been ready to go back to the Tories after such a mess. But by hanging on to power it was the Tories who looked tired, and accusations of sleaze – barely justified for a few individuals, very few of whom had been in government – stuck and Blair won his landslide. He went to the palace on the day we were cremating my mother and so politics seemed very unimportant that day, but I was aware that the country was ready for change and its expectations were too high. People projected their own aspirations on the chameleon Blair and he could only disappoint. General Election May 1997: Reigate Party Candidate Votes: Conservative – Crispin Blunt, 21,123, 43.8 per cent, -13.7 per cent; Labour – Andrew Howard, 13,382, 27.8 per cent, +10.3 per cent; Liberal Democrats – Peter Samuel, 9,615, 20.0 per cent, -4.1 per cent; Referendum Party – Sir George Gardiner, 3,352, 7.0 per cent, N/A; Independent (politician) – Richard Higgs, 412, 0.9 per cent, N/A; UK Independence – Stephen Smith, 290, 0.6 per cent, N/A. **Majority** 7,741, 16.0 per cent; **turnout** 48,174, 74.4 per cent. Conservative gain from Referendum Party, swing -12.

After four years of Blair's spin and Gordon Brown's stealth taxes, not enough people were changing their minds. We had moved to Harpenden in Peter Lilley's constituency. For the first time in my life I joined the Conservative party, so disgusted was I with the Blair government. Coca joined with me and we supported the party at a number of primarily social events while never becoming active canvassers. General Election June 2001: Hitchin and Harpenden Party Candidate Votes: Conservative – Peter Lilley, 21,271, 47.3 per cent, +1.5 per cent; Labour – Alan Amos, 14,608, 32.5 per cent, -0.6 per cent; Liberal Democrats – John Murphy, 8,076, 18.0 per cent, -2.1 per cent; UK Independence – John Saunders,

606, 1.3 per cent, N/A; Independent – Peter Rigby, 363, 0.8 per cent, N/A. **Majority** 6,663, 14.8 per cent; **turnout** 44,924, 66.9 per cent; -11.1 per cent. Conservative hold.

By the 2005 election we had had the war crime of Iraq. Many left the Labour Party and looked for alternatives to support, but the Conservatives had also wrongly supported the war and could not be the beneficiaries of the mood in the country. The numbers meant that Blair won a third term with only 35 per cent of the vote on a 59 per cent turnout, and so only 21 per cent of the total electorate had actually voted for him. We are paying the price for this scandal to this day. General Election 2005: Hitchin and Harpenden Party Candidate Votes: Conservative – Peter Lilley, 23,627, 49.9 per cent, +2.6 per cent; Liberal Democrats – Hannah Hedges, 12,234, 25.8 per cent, +7.8 per cent; Labour – Paul Orrett, 10,499, 22.2 per cent, -10.3 per cent; UK Independence – John Saunders, 828, 1.7 per cent, +0.4 per cent; Independent – Edward Rigby, 199, 0.4 per cent, +0.4 per cent. **Majority** 11,393, 24.0 per cent; **turnout** 47,387, 70.5 per cent, +3.6 per cent. Conservative hold.

(Note: I have not updated this thread as the politics of recent years is too raw. I think it helps to have some distance between one's reflections and the actual events. I stand by what I wrote here, particularly about Tony Blair, but the behaviour of all the parties and their leaders in recent years has severely damaged the British people's trust in our great political institutions.)

Being Right

"The minority is always right."

An Enemy of the People – Henrik Ibsen

"The greatest lesson in life is to know that even fools are right sometimes."

Sir Winston Churchill

February 2003

Two years ago, before the second Gulf War began, Tony Blair was trying to convince the British people that they were under immediate threat from Saddam Hussein's weapons of mass destruction and that this justified the war. Two-thirds of the British people believed him. Now no weapons have been found, the Americans have given up looking for them, and less than a third still believe the Prime Minister over this issue.

I never believed him and was certain, not just doubtful, that no such weapons would be found. I was clear that Blair wanted to fight the war anyway and was looking for an excuse. I was sure that he had perverted the instruments of British government to get his way. It is the fifth war that he has fought in six years as Prime Minister. He has dropped more bombs than any previous British Prime Minister, including Winston Churchill. On this, as on many things, I know that I am right.

Being right is difficult. Just saying it sounds arrogant. And I am certainly not saying that I am always right. Far from it, I believe a substantial part of wisdom is to have the knowledge to know that you are

Threads and Patches

not always right. But on many occasions I find myself in a minority but know that I am right. This is frustrating.

Sometimes it is because the majority is easily led, as over Iraq. The big lie is believed and the more it is told the more it is believed. Both Goebbels and Orwell taught us this. Sometimes it is because the majority is not capable of understanding the truth. This is particularly true of matters of science and mathematics as when statistics are perverted or the doctrine of the precautionary principle is invoked. An example was CJD. When a few people died of a human variant of the disease supposedly linked to mad cow disease, the numbers were extrapolated to scare people into thinking that an epidemic was on its way. No such epidemic happened. To date less than 200 people have died of this variant in 10 years, when we kill that many every two weeks on the road. No such link has been demonstrated. I was certain that it would not be and was anxious to eat more beef to demonstrate this.

Such examples call into question the principle of democracy. Democracy was invented as an alternative to rule by an individual (autocracy) or by an elite (aristocracy, theocracy) in ancient Athens. However, the demos, the people who ruled, were the property-owning male citizens. It is a very recent invention to extend this principle to all adults and arguably it is not fully tested. Churchill said that it was a poor system but better than all the alternatives, and that probably is right, but in a modern democracy the vote of the uneducated, ignorant individual with no stake in the system except claims on its benefits has as much power as the educated, intelligent individual who has made commitments to the system.

Knowledge and judgement are, of course, different. Trivial Pursuit is a game that tests our general knowledge. In general I perform well in this game and rarely lose it. In this sense I am often right, but the question is binary. Either I know the answer or I don't. Another game of general knowledge is *Who Wants To Be a Millionaire*? This TV game gives the contestant three "lifelines" to help him on his way to a million pounds. One, "50.50", simply removes two out of four possible answers and thus increases his chances of being right with a random guess to "50.50". Another gives him the opportunity to "phone a friend" and consult the friend, who has thirty seconds to answer, presumably to stop him looking it up in a reference book or on his phone. The third gives him the opportunity to "ask the audience". The members of the audience each have an electronic pad on which they can express their choice of answer. Here the majority are usually right, particularly in the earlier rounds when the questions are indeed of general knowledge. This kind of example is sometimes used to justify the idea that the majority knows best, but it confuses knowledge with wisdom.

Common sense is not common. The majority taste is banal. The majority bet on the lottery when a clever person can win at gambling by betting on his knowledge of the form against the market. I was introduced to horse racing by Allan Leonard. Allan knew much about racing and taught me some of it. I found that picking winners is not particularly difficult although backing them to make money is. I rarely bet away from the course and then only on the big races where you could be sure that every horse was at its fittest and every trainer and jockey would try his best. I often backed the winners of the Derby and even the Grand National this way. At the course, one had the advantage of seeing the horse in the flesh and sometimes the appearance of a horse in the paddock persuaded me to change my bet. Over the years I kept a record and won more than I lost, but not enough to repay the effort and not enough to keep it going.

The Stock Exchange is also a form of gambling. Most investment professionals tell us that over the long term, equity investments have outperformed all others. But this is only true in retrospect. It is only true if we eliminate all the failures. However, if we had invested in the top companies in the 1920s, most of those have disappeared today. To make money we would have had to switch our investments on a frequent basis. In other words we would have had to actively manage our investments, or pay someone to do this. The fund managers charge for this purpose, and are rewarded even when they fail. I believe the Stock Exchange is a giant casino and few people in it know when they are right. One study shows that 85 per cent of fund managers fail to beat the index!

As an exercise I selected ten stocks that I thought would appreciate during the year. As a control factor I selected ten stocks in the same sectors that I thought would perform badly. I used my knowledge of the companies, their management, their marketing, to make my choices. Of my ten to follow, nine share prices grew well during the year. Of my ten to avoid only two grew. I thus proved to myself that I could select such stocks but this is like picking winners in horse racing. It is not that difficult. It is much more difficult to make money at the process.

By the same token, as the Internet boom was reaching its height in 1999, I published an article in *Market Leader*, a publication of the Marketing Society of which I am a Fellow (see the full article under the heading 'The Threats and Opportunities of the Internet' on page 230). My contention was that the Internet was grossly overrated and that many of the predictions for it would not happen or certainly would not happen at the pace or on the scale that was being forecast. Such a view was very much in the minority, yet if I had had the skill, the knowledge and the courage I could have made a fortune betting against the Stock Market at that time.

Instead I found myself recruited to head up a technology company whose own valuation was extraordinary. I differentiated NXT from all the Internet companies as it offered a real technology, which could be differentiated. In this I was right. My error was to assume that the Stock Market had reached the same rational conclusion. Instead it irrationally applied its own twisted logic of supply and demand for the few shares that are being traded on any one day as the way to value a company. At its peak, NXT was valued at over £1.5 billion when it was losing money on sales of less than £12 million. Of this turnover, the majority came from a division that had been sold to help finance the rest. The ones who were right were those who sold out at the top; that included my predecessor as Chief Executive who had exercised share options to a value over £20 million through a so-called family trust.

Such career decisions are often fraught with difficulty but must be looked at in the round. My decision to leave Sony in 1998 may have been correct but to join Pentland at the same time was certainly incorrect from a career point of view. However, as a result the family moved to Harpenden where we have never been happier.

Of even greater importance, my decision to go to Chile in 1981 did not really work out as the economy collapsed the following year and wiped out the business I ran for Mars. But because I went to Chile I found Coca and I have never been more right than when I asked her to marry me.

I've Got a Little List

> As some day it may happen that a victim must be found
> I've got a little list – I've got a little list.
> Of society offenders who might well be under ground
> And who never would be missed – who never would be missed.
> They'll none of them be missed.
>
> William Schwenk Gilbert

I have never really kept a diary. There was a brief period when as a presumptuous youth, full of unwarranted self-belief, I started to keep a diary full of pretentious thoughts and ridiculous predictions. This was in January 1965; it was about the same time that I started writing equally pretentious poetry. I remember writing my prospective entry in *Who's Who*. Something along the lines of Oxford, called to the bar, MP, Minister, Prime Minister, that sort of thing. I did take a degree in Law from Oxford but I am glad to say the rest of it never happened. I reached the pages of Debretts' *People of Today*, the poor man's *Who's Who*, and I'll settle for that.

My mother kept a comprehensive diary for many years. She was an excellent correspondent and kept in touch with many of her family and friends to the very end of her life. Her diary was a fascinating compendium of minutiae and observation, description of events and milestones, the weather and journey times. Her memory was excellent and I am sure that the act of committing all this to the written page aided this just as a student retains the lecture better by taking notes.

Threads and Patches

Instead of a diary I have kept copious lists. I have lists of everything: books read, plays seen, places visited; for a number of years I kept a list of movies seen and then Halliwell published his wonderful work on all the movies he had seen and it became simpler to just mark off the ones I had seen.

Freud would no doubt say that this propensity to keep lists marks some deep psychosis, probably as a result of sexual repression, or perhaps just inadequate toilet training. But then I would put Herr Freud at the top of my list of frauds.

I think it is more to do with the need to complete the challenges of life before it is over. Some of this can never be done, some can. I cannot visit all the countries of the world but I can make a good attempt, and it is over 75 to date. I can never see all the games that Manchester United play but I can keep a record and thus prove my tribal loyalty. I can read every published work by Dickens and Wodehouse, see every opera by Verdi and Wagner.

The train spotter sets out to collect a batch of numbers. That has never appealed to me but I seek to collect a batch of experiences. Some of this is random. Some of this is planned. William Shakespeare wrote thirty-seven plays and I have seen every one in the theatre.

I have kept a list of every book I have read since school days and my current records go back to the 1970s. Again, as thousands of books are published every year and I read about sixty or seventy, then this is not about conquest or completion. Rather it is about a sense of balance in ensuring that I am reading well and not frittering the time away.

And that is the real motive. I said I do not keep a diary, but, of course, I do keep a business diary and have some sort of record back to 1980. Here the objective is to use limited time to the maximum advantage. This is not the motive of a Pepys or an Alan Clark. Their diaries are wonderful commentaries on the age they lived in as well as the part they played in that age.

The real enemy is time and the real challenge is to beat it. In the end you will never succeed. But on the way you can have a lot of fun and satisfaction in trying.

Immortality

"In the long run, we are all dead."

John Maynard Keynes

"I don't want to achieve immortality through my work.
I want to achieve immortality through not dying."

Woody Allen

People long for immortality, and if that is not on offer, then life after death. Most religions fit in with this longing and some are amazingly specific in what they offer. The scientist cannot reject this belief out of hand because there cannot be scientific proof in the accepted sense of that word, but I am certain that these beliefs are founded on nothing more than the wishful fantasy of the human. It is man who has created God, not the other way round.

The Christian dogma is quite interesting. The Old Testament was written in Hebrew but the New Testament was written in Greek, later translated into Latin, and then into many other languages. With each translation errors creep into the dogma. For example, nowhere in the New Testament in the original Greek does the word for immortal, ἀθάνατός, appear. Instead the word αἰωνίος is used. This is translated as everlasting which means something quite different. Indeed, some theologians think it means that Jesus was talking about a post-conversion state rather than a post-death state.

Threads and Patches

Before the bible was written and before the Christian era, a form of immortality had been achieved by the Pharaohs. They had sought immortality through the construction of their tombs. These were built at huge expense in terms of material and human life. Once dead, their bodies were mummified which prevented deterioration by exposure to damp and air. But most spectacularly, these tombs were built in a pyramid form of such size that they are still to be seen. As a result, modern archaeologists and historians have learnt what they can about these people and thus they have achieved a form of immortality.

More recently, great architects like Sir Christopher Wren have achieved similar immortality. Wren took thirty-five years to complete St Paul's Cathedral, an outstanding building by any definition. It was Wren's eldest son and heir, Christopher Wren, Jr., who wrote what is perhaps one of the most famous epitaphs of all time: "*Lector, Si Monumentum Requiris Circumspice*" ("Reader, if you seek his monument, look around").

One can think of Eiffel's Tower, Brunel's bridges and the palaces and castles of a host of Kings and Queens, Popes and Princes. Modern political leaders agonise about their legacy and write their memoirs to try and steer their followers in the direction it might be found.

Inventors achieve immortality through their inventions, everyone knows who discovered America, and Herr Alzheimer has achieved a form of immortality that he might wish we had all forgotten. Einstein is the scientist we have all heard of and most of us could probably quote $e=mc^2$ without being able to explain it. The Wright brothers were the first to fly, Roger Bannister to run a mile in less than four minutes, Neil Armstrong to take that small step onto the moon.

The apparent immortality of today's popular celebrities is no doubt ephemeral. Andy Warhol foretold this era with his prediction that "in the future everyone will have their fifteen minutes of fame". He could, no doubt, have gone further and predicted *Big Brother*. Mozart had his contemporaries, think of Salieri, but the passage of time is ruthless and it is only Mozart who has achieved immortality.

The most interesting character in this tale is Charles Darwin who both explained immortality and achieved it. Darwin's discovery, with the help of others, of the theory of evolution has led to what Richard Dawkins explains as *The Selfish Gene*. This means that actually there is part of us all which lives after our death, but here on earth, and in our progeny. Indeed, it is the very purpose of life, to reproduce and thus ensure the survival of the species. We die because we have achieved our purpose, to hand on our genes to the next generation.

> "He was the centre of the earth
> His words were bible to us all;
> But as we all are taught from birth,
> He found pride comes before a fall."
>
> Author, aged about 15

Edited July 2009
Re-edited September 2020